OUT OF THE BOX

MOSAICA PRESS

OUT OF THE BOX

**PARASHAH INSIGHTS TO
INSPIRE A CONVERSATION**

Doni Sausen, Ben Baruch, and Ryan Render
Based on the teachings of Rav Yair Halevi

In loving memory of

UNCLE YITZY CRAITENBERGER

יצחק בן חיים הלוי ז״ל

Whose passion for studying was passed onto his nephews and nieces.

In loving memory of my father

ר׳ משה בן ידידיה ז״ל

Whose passion for Torah and learning was only surpassed
by his love for prayer with a minyan.

שהחיינו וקיימנו לזמן הזה

Thank you

הרב דניאל משה

for being an inspiration to me and the entire Klal Yisrael.
May you continue to be a guiding light to all of us. We are truly blessed.

AUNT ROCHELLE AND UNCLE YOSSI
ELIZABETH, MELISSA, LAUREN, AND NICOLE TABBOUCHE

In honor of

RAV YAIR AND TANYA

for the impact they continue to make on all of Am Yisrael.

THE STEPNER FAMILY

Dearest Rebbi,
I can't thank you enough for sharing your light with me
and all of your students. I hope that this *sefer* is able to
capture some of that and share it with many others.
L'chaim al mayim,

BENJY SCHWARTZ

לכבוד הרב יאיה, תניה, וכל משפחת אייזנשטוק–הלוי שמזכירים
לכל אחד ואחד בעם ישראל את יכולתם, כחותם, ומטרתם בחיים.

משפחת שטרמן
תל אביב–יפו
שנת 47 לגאולה

Rebbi, thank you for showing and revealing
to me the קודש הקדשים in my life.

JACOB AND NECHAMA

In honor of

THE YEAR 1 CHOVAT BOYS

Keep rolling, Rebbi.

THE LASKO FAMILY

TABLE OF CONTENTS

PARSHIYOT

MOADIM

PREFACE

MOST OF US read a book to learn something new. The book has new information that we want to gain. This book has a little bit of a different orientation. It is meant to be a "start-up"—not in the regular sense of the word, but rather in that it is meant to be continued and developed. The book is like a springboard that can be used to create a new perspective and a fresh insight on what used to seem slightly irrelevant or not interesting. We want this book to be used like a key that will open up great places within you and your family at your Shabbat table.

Rav Yair says: My *rebbi*, Rav Re'em, asks a question: What is special about Torah learning, and what makes it different from all other areas of study? He answers that it's the difference between water in an ocean versus water in a pool.

True, they both have water. But the water in the ocean is the source of the relationship between sky and earth; the water there is beyond limits—like any relationship that breaks the boundaries of life. A pool is a defined expression of what is in the ocean; it shows an aspect of the eternal life in the ocean, but one that is limited and controlled by borders.

Books in their essence are like a pool: They give over information, but they lose out on the relationship. They give over ideas from one place to another, but the person in the other place belongs to a different part of the world—they have a different level of things they are looking at and looking for.

We want this book, as much as possible, to promote relationships that will hopefully be built from the ideas shared, in an open rather than a confining way.

So, we daven that these pages will turn into something limitless for every person who reads them—a few ingredients that will enable the reader to develop much better and greater ideas. We hope that you and your family build your own continuation of this book.

ACKNOWLEDGMENTS

TO BEN BARUCH and **Ryan Render,** I cannot thank you guys enough for not taking your feet off the pedal for even a second, and for believing in this dream with me to make it come true.

To the **Mosaica Team,** and specifically **Rabbi Doron Kornbluth,** for seeing this unique Torah not just as *divrei Torah*, but as life-changing messages.

"Ohhh, Rebbi, Rebbi, Rebbi"—to my *rebbi* and dearest friend, **Rav Yair,** who pushed me beyond limits. How grateful am I to no longer be woken up at 5:45 a.m. by the sound of a blasting shofar in my ear, a cold bucket of water over my head, or the piercing noise of your never-ending screech. But there's something about it that I miss. It shook off all the dust, and it allowed me to wake up and see the world. The everlasting effect is what continues to make me constantly realize that I am capable of anything.

To my **Mom,** thank you for always making my favorite desserts and for still loving me with all my decisions even if they change every other moment (Rutgers, Maryland, YU), and to **Yitz** for always offering help and assistance in any way you possibly can. We're so happy to have you join the family. It's hard having brothers who no matter how hard I try, I can just never outdo. **Aiden,** you have an understanding for the world, and will go forward with any task imaginable because you believe in it with all your heart. **Owen,** try slowing the growth rate on a physical and spiritual level (just kidding, *chas v'shalom*). Most tenth graders don't just fall in love with Judaism, but you are special, and no one can stop you from elevating as highly as you desire.

To **Bobby** and **Zeidy,** for being a guiding light in my life and being the most honest people I know. You two will always make sure my stomach is filled at max capacity, but the buttermilk pancakes will never be turned down.

To **Aunt Rochelle** and **Uncle Yossi**, thank you for giving me lifelong sisters in your girls, **Elizabeth**, **Melissa**, **Lauren**, and **Nikki**. To many more Friday night meals filled with laughs together!

To my newest family, **Mom** and **Ta**, who have loved me from the start like their very own. I feel so welcome and blessed to be a part of the crew starting with **Yitz**, **Gila**, **Judah**, **Ellie**, and **Nora** to **Dani** and all the way to **Mickey**, **Nina**, **Zev**, and **Noah**.

Thank You, **Hashem**, for blessing me with the strength and vision to spread Your light in this fashion. Please allow me to continue to be a messenger for You and Your holy nation. Thank You for leading me to my beautiful wife and laughing partner, **Sara**, who showed me that smiling in this world is allowed and encouraged. To many more ice-cream parties together, and one day *b'ezrat Hashem* with our **future children**, who were the driving force in all of this. Hopefully, one day, you guys will read this and know that it is all for you. We should all merit in seeing good things and Mashiach in our days!

Doni Sausen

Elul 5782

I'D LIKE TO ACKNOWLEDGE first the three great leaders of our generation who spent thousands of hours turning random Torah pieces into a book.

Rav **Doni Sausen** for bringing full tears to my eyes.

Rabbi **Ben Baruch** for listening through the words.

For Reb **Ryan Render** for making thoughts into words.

I want all my **students** to know they are all-stars.

So many friends and parents who support this *sefer*, our Yeshiva TVA / Chovat HaTalmidim and every need of Am Yisrael.

It's important to thank the **Piaseczna Rebbe** for dedicating so much of his time a hundred years ago, so that I, as a young sixteen-year-old, would find a truly aware and real Rebbe.

I'm blessed with a wide family of grandparents, siblings, cousins, nieces, and nephews who combine the intensity and fun of Judaism together.

I have a great present from Hashem to have **in-laws** who treat me like a child and unite *chessed* and Torah.

I admire my **Abba** and **Imma** for helping me have the confidence to be different and connected at the same time.

I want my children, **Ohr Eytan Yehuda**, **Adiel Raz Shlomo**, and **Roni Shir Yocheved** to know that they are my source of happiness.

Above all, my wife, **Tanya**, who, in our first sixteen years together, has given me confidence, balance, patience, inner happiness, and a true best friend.

And within everything, **Hashem,** Who has given us His Torah, His world, His land, His hidden sparks, to feel truly hugged and supported by His endless good.

Yair HaLevi Eisenstock
Elul 5782

INTRODUCTION

THIS BOOK PRESENTS many ideas on the parashah of the week. Many of these ideas were taught by the *Sefat Emet* in the years 1871–1902; many of them are from the Piaseczna Rebbe, from his *divrei Torah* in the years before the Shoah in his *sefer*, *Chovat HaTalmidim*, and his other writings from the Warsaw Ghetto; other ideas are from Rav Kook. The different ideas attempt to bring the parashah of the week expressed through the light of Chassidic masters to our Shabbat tables. Through these teachings on the parashah, we are trying to give the people who are reading these ideas in preparation for Shabbat three keys to three great palaces:

1. The palace of Shabbat
2. The palace of family
3. The palace of *Chassidut*

Why these three? And how can we unlock these three palaces?

THE PALACE OF SHABBAT

Why Shabbat? Our modern era has opened many opportunities for us. But with great potential comes great danger. One of the dangers is the loss of Shabbat, and on a deeper level, a Shabbat lifestyle.

Often in the modern era, quantity takes precedence over quality, as numbers are what matter while names are forgotten. Progress demands results, and the process has become nonsense. We have so much speed, but yet have lost sight of the destination; we have thousands of gadgets to save us time, but never seem to be satisfied with the extra time we've received. We have more titles, and less date nights. Image has become the picture—and the picture has become one color. We've built towers, but might have forgotten the building blocks. We have so much FaceTime but almost no face to face. We have, and we have, and

1

we have—but we can't enjoy what we have. We are looking downward more than forward, because our center is our phone and people are secondary. We can find anything on Google, but we can't seem to find one relationship. People have thousands of "friends" on Facebook and feel lonelier than Noach in the *teivah*.

Being faced with this reality, Hashem created a remedy, already from the beginning of existence. Progress is great; work is special; quantities are needed—on condition that they are the branches of something much more important: the quality relationships we possess. The relationship between us and Hashem, us and our families. The first day that Adam and Eve experienced—since they were last to be created on the sixth day of Creation—was Shabbat. Why was their first day a day of rest? They hadn't worked for six days yet to earn this "sleep and bliss." But on a very deep and profound level, Hashem was educating them, and us, to rethink what Shabbat is for man. It wasn't our seventh day of existence—it was our first—therefore, teaching us that this isn't a day of rest, but rather a day of direction. It's not a gas station because the tank is empty from a long drive; rather, it's a gas station you go to before a road trip—where you go to get direction (before GPS came around), to buy a coffee, to check the tires and fill the water and oil. Shabbat is our starting point; it's when we figure out *why* we are working, *why* we are earning our salaries. It's when we recognize who we want to drive with and how each thing we have is what we desire, and that we don't need all the great miles and views to give us bliss—it's right here. From this we can go out to the world of progress and speed with clarity. We can give to the world from a place of strength and not run after the world from a place of need.

This is why we call it a Shabbat lifestyle. Shabbat is also a mindset. It's a mindset we create on Shabbat itself, but also very similarly in our davening of *Shemoneh Esreh*. We go back three times a day—to this moment where movement can wait and success can be on hold. We re-enter the Shabbat lifestyle. It is a moment when one becomes aware of the whole picture, a moment that gives room for breathing to be for the sake of enjoyment and not just to catch one's breath.

Also, on a practical level, our advice is not to read this at the Shabbat table, but a few hours before Shabbat. The reason for this is based on a great idea taught by Rav Soloveitchik. He said we have so many "Shabbat Jews" but no "Erev Shabbat Jews." With these words, the Rav was teaching that we tend to focus on keeping Shabbat but not preparing for it.

Baruch Hashem, growing up in Israel, Friday was our Sunday. For sure, on many levels a Sunday would be nice, but the Friday off is what turned Shabbat on. Friday was the day my *abba* would bring home chocolate croissants; it was the day that there was special music in the house, the day that everyone was fighting about cleaning, and also calmly peeling potatoes. But Shabbat really started on Friday. Once I had the privilege to marry Tanya, Shabbat would begin Thursday night with cutting vegetables and stirring pots for Shabbat. When we moved to Yerushalayim and the lines at the supermarket became longer and longer, shopping for Shabbat became earlier and earlier, and I found myself preparing for Shabbat on Monday: the day the lines seemed to have an end.

On a certain level this is what the Rav was teaching: we must do everything possible to make Shabbat our beginning.

There is a famous saying that says, "*Mi she'tarach b'erev Shabbat yochal b'Shabbat*—One who takes pains [toils] on Shabbat eve will eat on Shabbat," which on a deeper level means that Shabbat with its prohibitions of cooking and creating is forcing us to prepare, to enter in earlier.[1] To make sure we have a Shabbat playlist we are listening to, and to have special *minhagim* on Friday or even Thursday that help us kindle the Shabbat lifestyle—not only to prepare for Shabbat, but to continue from Shabbat.

To continue—in the army, the most painful sentence was "*l'chol Shabbat yesh Motzaei Shabbat.*" It was meant to scare us. Don't get excited about your twenty-four hours off, because we will make you run, sweat, and cry right after every short vacation you get from the army on Shabbat. So, I once told my commander when he yelled that every Shabbat has a Motzaei Shabbat, "You are right," and we started dancing and singing Shabbat *zemirot* late into Motzaei Shabbat. Every Shabbat that is real and full will define Motzaei Shabbat and will give us direction for the week.

---

1   *Avodah Zarah* 3a.

The first palace we want to try and give the key to in this book is the greatest present in the world: "The Shabbat lifestyle." And this book can help us prepare for the Shabbat table and extend it into the week with opportunities which continue out from the book.

THE PALACE OF FAMILY

Why family? Once upon a time, back in the 1980s, there was a TV show in Japan called *National Dilemma*. The show would show a dilemma to the nation, and people would call in (not text, and with a real house phone with a cord) to give their answer. So, one of the dilemmas was: There is a house burning down, and in it are the prime minister and your spouse. You have the time to only save one. Who do you save? Eighty-three percent decided to save the prime minister. The reason for this decision was selflessness. Saving your wife helps you; saving the prime minister saves millions.

It sounds extremely altruistic, but it is also the antithesis of Judaism. Our nation is built in *Sefer Shemot* and our family is built in *Sefer Bereishit*. The foundation of our nation is our family, not our nation. The way we celebrate the night of our national independence is on Seder night—not with the nation, and not in the streets, but rather surrounded by our families. Our families are our link to our nation. For us, this isn't a dilemma; without your wife there is no nation. The question doesn't even start, because the prime minister is only a prime minister if one sees his wife and family as the core and the center of anything that could and will happen with the entire nation.

Our center today has become our offices, and our homes have become a comfortable place to sleep in. The family unit has become "annoying," and a waste of our "precious time." Since "time is money," family has become the problem and commitment to the regular acts of life have become costly in the "killing time" mentality. Fast food is our go to since it will give us more quality time in front of our computer. This reality is so important to internalize and change as quickly as possible.

How do we want this book to help this circle?

The greatest family circle we have is centered around Shabbat. The idea of our providing opening questions and quick sentences for each piece on the parashah is so that they should be a point of conversation for our families. The ending mission for each piece is designed to provide a possible way of thinking together as a family and incorporating the ideas to ourselves and to our lives.

THE PALACE OF CHASSIDUT

The concept of *Chassidut* is used often. There are many ways to try and explain the idea of *Chassidut*, and one of the easiest ways is through the psychology of Torah. *Chassidut* is a way of trying to understand not only what happened in the Torah—not seeing it as just as a book of facts, laws, and things that happened—but rather, trying to understand why things are said, how they are said, and especially in what way they are relevant to us now. The Torah is not just a recollection of what happened there and then, but its words are a link and a connection to each of us individually now.

To explain why we have chosen to connect to the palace of *Chassidut*, I will share a story. My daughter, "princess" Roni, is four years old. She was playing with her friend from kindergarten. He only wanted to play with cars, when the regular toys for Roni are dolls and unicorns. Roni, with her creativity, gave all the cars family titles, just like she does with her dolls. She took something which was foreign to her and made it relatable.

The Torah is something that is beyond this world, bigger than our reality. *Chassidut* is such a great tool for our generation. It connects us to otherwise distant ideas. It builds a bridge between where we are and where Hashem is. The bridge that *Chassidut* builds is so essential, so needed, especially in our generation which struggles with mental health issues. Finding inner-joy through *Chassidut* can help us resolve these issues by serving as a channel to infuse our personal lives with the endless light of Hashem through the Torah.

HOW DO WE USE CHASSIDUT IN THIS BOOK?

The structure of the book is based on *Chassidut* on the concepts of *chochmah*, *binah*, and *daat*; it goes through the journey of a full relationship with many ideas in the Torah. The ideas themselves are either directly from *Chassidut* or following the Chassidic mindset.

PARSHIYOT

NO FEAR, ALL PATIENCE

WHEN WE BEGIN *Sefer Bereishit*, we can feel very frustrated, because in every parashah we can enter into a seemingly infinite number of ideas and teachings. So, we will just focus on one, though there are so many.

The first word of the Torah is *Bereishit*, and there are books and books that have been written about this word. For example, the *Tikkunei Zohar* writes an extensive amount just about this one word.

Then there is the explanation of the *Sefat Emet*, which examines the letters of the word *Bereishit* and, at the same time, also gives us a very deep understanding of the purpose of Creation. What this means is that if you look at the word "*Bereishit*," you will note that it has six letters: *beis, reish, aleph, shin, yud,* and *tav*. Based on this, the *Sefat Emet* divides these letters into two words: if you take the *yud, reish,* and *aleph,* it spells *yerei*, meaning, "you will see," while the remaining letters of *shin, bet, tav* spell out Shabbat.

He says that the idea of Creation, which is hiding within the word of *Bereishit*, is seeing Shabbat. But what does the *Sefat Emet* really mean when he says that the idea of *Bereishit* is *seeing* Shabbat?

It could be that he is saying that one of the things we don't recognize is that Hashem built a world that is not Shabbat. The world starts off from *tohu va'vohu*, void and unformed, which is essentially chaos. Anyone who begins any journey, any creation, and any business endeavor always begins with this concept of *tohu va'vohu*. And just like the world started with chaos, so too, any relationship and anything we build begins with *tohu va'vohu*.

We see this sometimes at the end, but Hashem is saying that the essential nature of the world is that it is *presented* to us as one of confusion and uncertainty. Only at the end, after six days of Hashem building the world, does He say that it is a journey and a process. Hashem could have just built the world in one day, but He didn't. He took six days. If Hashem built it for us in six days, then it would have taken us sixty or maybe six hundred or even six thousand years to build the world.

What Hashem is saying is that the goal is to understand that the idea of *tohu va'vohu* is a privilege, that chaos is a privilege, that questions are an opportunity, and that struggles are not only problems. There is something that is enabling us to *seek* Shabbat and to look *yerei Shabbat*, and that is the end of *perek aleph* where we get into *perek beit* where Hashem creates Shabbat. So, what the *Sefat Emet* is saying is that in the first word of the Torah, Hashem reveals to us that the greatest problem is fear. Like Moreinu v'Rabbeinu Reb Nachman explains, "והעיקר לא לפחד כלל—The main point is not to be afraid at all." Don't let yourself be afraid because everything is an ingredient.

Tohu va'vohu is an ingredient, and it's an ingredient that says there needs to be a journey. So, what we have to learn from the *Sefat Emet*'s idea of the word *Bereishit* being the letters of *yerei Shabbat* is that we are our own enemy because we don't have vision. We don't have the vision of Shabbat; therefore, we are afraid of *Tohu va'vohu* and we are afraid of problems. However, once we have vision, once we have Shabbat, and once we are able to see that there is a perfect world, then we will not only be able to have vision, but we will have patience. We will not be afraid, and we will be able to enter into the chaos and start organizing it. Start to listen to it. Start to embrace it. Start to internalize it.

The berachah, as we walk into *Bereishit*, is that we're going to meet a broken reality: brothers that fight, Kayin and Hevel who fought against each other, the generation of *Migdal Bavel* which fought against God, and Avraham Avinu who tried so hard to succeed but a lot of things didn't go his way. All of this along with many more conflicts in *Sefer Bereishit*. The *Sefat Emet* is teaching us that in the first word, we can learn the essence of this *sefer*: That if you have the image of Shabbat, if you have a clear vision of the future, if you love the idea of where you want to go, then not only will you get there, but everything on the way will become a blessing.

Parashat Noach

HEALTHY PROGRESS

> "Actions that last are a result of awareness
> [in connection to time, others, and future impact]."
>
> "Success that is secondary to a primary vision will be eternal."

OPENING QUESTIONS

1. How do you perceive Noach's character?
2. What is the difference between success that is selfish and success that is selfless?
3. Why do you think the generation of the *Mabul* all drowned?

LEARNING CONVERSATION

Before we begin to enter into the story of Noach, there's a concept that we need to explore. The world that we live in is very focused on progress and accomplishments. From a young age, when our kids enter first grade, there are already tests to measure their accomplishments and progress. So, a question we can ask and think about with our families and ourselves is: What is the definition of successful progress? Progress, in its essence, is positive. Hashem wants us to build, to create, and to do a lot of great things. But the question is how do we know when our progress is healthy and how do we know when is it destructive? I think that we can learn the answer from *Parashat Noach*.

The *Zohar Hakadosh* has an incredible sentence in its remarks on *Parashat Noach* that needs to be understood. The *Tikkunei Zohar* states that "נח הוא בחינת שבת—The essence of Noach is the concept of

Shabbat."[1] The question that we need to ask about the *Zohar* is: Where do we see a link between Noach and Shabbat?

If we think about it, we will discover that there are connections between the character of Noach and the definition of Shabbat. We can see this by focusing on: (a) Noach's name; (b) Noach's identity; (c) Noach's relationship with society; and (d) Shabbat as the only day with a blessing.

A. Noach's Name

The name of Noach stems from the root *menuchah*.[2] The idea of *menuchah* is relaxation. It is where I'm not doing, and I'm not acting. Instead, I'm internalizing all the external elements that are in front of me: family, home, and community.

Let's say on Shabbat someone was offered a business deal of a million dollars, and with those million dollars they can save five different schools and six hospitals. Yet comes along Shabbat and says, "You have to take a step back. You can't create. I don't want you to leave your home. I don't want you to leave your community. I am asking you on this day to focus on the most important parts of your life journey." Similar to this idea of Shabbat, Noach's name is connected to this idea of passivity and taking a step backward, not forward. The world in Noach's days had so much progress, so many animals, and so many people. In Noach's time, he decided to take a step back. This is the first link between Noach and Shabbat.

B. Noach's Identity

The second link is his identity and his character. The identity of Noach is doing what Hashem says. Period. Nothing else. No questions, no additions, and no added intentions. *L'havdil*, like the motto of Nike: "Just Do It." Noach did what Hashem told him to do. Hashem said to build a *teivah*, so he built a *teivah*. Hashem said to save his children,

---

1   *Tikkunei Zohar* 70, p. 131a; *Zohar*, vol. I, 58b.

2   It is interesting to learn that the reason given for Noach's name in *Bereishit* 5:29 means that it should have been מנחם, from the root of consoling, but that is a different *shiur* in and of itself.

so he saved his children. And because Hashem did not say to save the world, he didn't save the world.

Noach was focused on one thing and one thing only, and whatever he was told is what he did. And similarly, Shabbat is not about you and it's not about you creating. It is about you receiving the responsibility which was given to you. Noach, like Shabbat, is the acceptance of responsibility.

C. Noach's Relationship with Society

The third thing is that Noach's focus is not on humanity. The sentence, "ויעש נח ככל אשר צוה אתו אלוקים"—Noach did so; just as God commanded him, so he did," reveals that his actions and his focus were only on Hashem, period.[3] His focus was not on humanity. His focus was not on people. And his focus was not on progress. Instead, his focus was on the essence of what it means to have a relationship with Hashem.

D. Shabbat as the Only Day with a Blessing

The fourth link, I think, is something very essential. The only day of the week that received a berachah during Creation is Shabbat. Reflecting on this, the *Sefat Emet* asks how this makes any sense, since, compared to the rest of the other six days of Creation, there was no progress on Shabbat!

On the first day, Hashem created light. On the second day, Hashem created the sky. On the third day, Hashem created the earth. On the fourth day, Hashem created the sun and the moon and all the constellations. But on Shabbat, He created nothing! So, we would have thought that Shabbat shouldn't receive a berachah. Shabbat is different from the other days. There is no progress made on Shabbat. Yet, it is specifically Shabbat that received the berachah, although admittedly it doesn't make so much sense.

Yet Noach was the same. Noach was different from his generation. The generation of Noach is defined by "ותמלא הארץ חמס—The earth was filled with lawlessness."[4] There are many ways to translate this, but let's

---

3   *Bereishit* 6:22.
4   *Bereishit* 6:11.

take it on a simple level. The world is focused on *l'malot*, filling and filling and filling. They were focused on doing, acting, and working. And you look at the world the next day and it's gone. For 120 years, Noach built the *teivah*. But that was it. Noach was passive, like Shabbat when we don't do anything, and we rest. He didn't do anything, but for some reason, he became the continuation of the world. The *Sefat Emet* says, "אף כי בחינת זו קיפוח היגיון," meaning that this concept is the opposite of logic![5] You would have thought that the world and generation of Noach would have been so successful. They were so active. They were doing, and they were acting, and they probably got a 101 percent on every single test, and they probably had seven university degrees, and they probably were able to conquer every single business!

Yet with all of their progress, they lost it all. Noach was the antithesis and the opposite of his generation. He didn't do, and he didn't act, but he lived with *menuchah* with a focused reality, not a progressive one, and he was the one to continue the generations of humanity in the world. The *Sefat Emet* explains why this is, the עיקר, the main point, that "התולדות תלוים בזה—The generations are dependent on this." Progress is essential, but the root of healthy progress is having a vision—a vision not of what you're doing, but of why you're doing it. I've been *zocheh* in the last few months, *b'ezrat Hashem*, to be in the administration here at Ohr Chaim. I've been given the *zechut* to try and help out the Yeshiva Bnei Akiva, *b'ezrat Hashem*, next year. A lot of the time, my focus is: How do I get more students to get off their phones? My focus is: How do I get more students to put on and love their tefillin? And what the *Sefat Emet* is teaching through Noach is that our focus on numbers and quantity is destroying our students. It's destroying our identities, and

---

5   There is a similar concept between Yaakov and Eisav. Eisav begins with a name that defines him, with the *bechorah* and with berachah conceptually. In contrast, Yaakov's name is dependent—he was holding onto the heel of his brother with nothing of his own. He had no name of his own, as he wasn't the first born and wasn't supposed to get the berachah. At the end, it all flipped. Eisav's second name is Edom; he was dependent on his brother's soup. He has ended up losing his *bechorah* and his berachah. But Yaakov's second name is Yisrael: *yashar-el*. His own identity, his own name, has the *bechorah*. Yaakov started with Shabbat and ended with everything; Eisav started with progress and ended up with nothing.

we're not so different from the generation of Noach. We are *l'malot*, and *l'malot*, and *l'malot*, and we fill our time, and we fill our days. All of that is essential, on condition that it is secondary. But the question is: Do you realize that it *starts* from Shabbat? It starts from letting go. It starts from realizing that it's not about what you're doing, but about why you want to do what you're doing.

The berachah we have for this Shabbat, as we enter into the *Mabul* of Noach, is that we should realize and understand that the answer for healthy progress is that progress that is goal oriented is destructive. If the goal is progress only, and the goal is Ivy League, and the goal is numbers, and the goal is degrees, and how many zeros do we have in our salaries or whatever it is—that is not creation, that is destruction. What we learn from Noach is that progress must begin from a place of "I recognize that I'm not the center." Noach understands, like Shabbat, that he isn't the center. If you come from that perspective, we can overcome selfishness. Once we aren't just focused on our progress then there will be eternal growth.

We should be *zocheh* with our families to really focus on each other this Shabbat, so that we can realize that eternal progress is knowing to let go of what is outside and go back home—to let go of the sukkah which represents the outside world and the progressive world, with all of the great animals that we were sacrificing at the Beit Hamikdash—to let go, and go back home. Then when you go back home, you will understand your vision and that your progress isn't selfish, rather selfless—and you will understand that the success we have during the week is independent of other people's perception of us.

LIVING THE LEARNING

Make a special playlist for Erev Shabbat that will make Shabbat more special.

Parashat Noach

YOU'RE JUST SOMETHING

B'EZRAT HASHEM, as we enter *Parashat Noach*, the story is seemingly very obvious. We know about the flood, the sin, and the final conclusion: the world being flooded. But, a lot of people do not understand the end of the story, when Noach had to figure out when he was going to reenter the world, when he was going to leave the comfort zone of the *teivah*, ark, which contained everything he needed—food, family, self, and Hashem.

When he left the *teivah*, he would be going out into the struggles of life. What is interesting is that Noach sent out birds four different times; he sent the dove and the raven. But, at what time did Noach realize that he could leave his comfort zone and go out from the *teivah*?

The final time he sent the bird out, the Torah says "ולא יספה שוב אליו עוד—And it did not return to him anymore."[1] Oftentimes, when we learn this story, we think that the dove was able to live on its own, and that then Noach knew that he could leave the *teivah*. But the Torah emphasizes *"V'lo yasfah shuv eilav."*

The times Noach sent the birds and they returned back to him they were dependent on Noach. There was only one experience, one sending of the bird, where it says *"V'lo yasfah shuv eilav,"* thereby saying that they did not need him anymore. They put Noach in his place and said to him, "You might have thought you were going out into the world because you're the center, but I can survive without you, Noach. I can thrive without you, and I can succeed without you." Only then did Noach

---

1   *Bereishit* 8:12.

realize that he could go out into the world. What he had to realize was that what made the world fall apart was that everyone thought they were everything—that they were the ones that knew about business, law, Torah, and about *chessed*—that without them the world could not survive. What they failed to remember is that man was created last in all of Creation. In *Masechta Sanhedrin* 30b, the Gemara says that there are two reasons why man was created last. One is to show him that everything was made for him, but the other is to remind him that he is not so significant, because even cows and birds were created before him.

We live in times when we very often speak about this first message—that we are significant, powerful, and meaningful, that we have thousands of friends on Facebook, and even more on LinkedIn. Yet none of us realize that what enabled the world to survive was when Noach understood that while he was something, he was not everything.

My berachah is that we should enter into the sadness of *Parashat Noach*, that we see the world destroyed, but not only through seeing the pain of destruction. We must also analyze the reasons for that very destruction, the reason that we thought we were "the," that we were everything, that we were the reason and the cause. We used others. We stepped on other people. And so the *yonah*, dove, taught Noach "*V'lo yasfah shuv eilav*—I can do this without you." We need to realize that sometimes we are not the center, the full picture, and all the colors of the story. This will enable the story to become the best story ever— a bestseller.

Parashat Lech Lecha

STOP SUCCEEDING, START TRYING

Rav Yair talks about the identity of Avraham, the way the Sefat Emet sees it, and how it's connected to our generation and smartphones.

"Walking toward is natural; walking inward is special."

"There are two ways of walking. One is walking to progress. The second is walking through the success."

OPENING QUESTIONS

1. What do you think made Avraham special?
2. Why was Hashem's first command to Avraham *"Lech lecha"*?
3. What is the difference between a goal-oriented mind and a process-oriented mind? How do these orientations impact one's character?

LEARNING CONVERSATION

In *Parashat Lech Lecha*, we meet Avraham Avinu. So much has been said, and so much has been written about Avraham who was an incredible character as well as an incredible visionary. But what enabled Avraham to become who he was?

The first word said by God to Avraham was *lech*, go, and this can be seen as being much more than a command. In fact, the *Sefat Emet* understands this word as capturing the core essence of Avraham's character and uniqueness, "כי הוא נקרא אדם—because he is called *adam*."

Avraham, similar to mankind, is a *mehalach*, a walker. But what does it mean that mankind should be defined by this act of Avraham, this act of walking? Surely even animals walk?!

Two possible understandings of the definition of a character as a walker is on two levels: The story immediately before Avraham Avinu is Migdal Bavel. The people of the generation of Migdal Bavel feared "*pen nafutz*," lest we shall be scattered all over the world.[1] What does it mean when they say this? They were saying that "We do not want to disperse! We do not want to be in different places! We all want to be in one valley together and united!" You could call it communism, you could call it socialism, you could call it whatever you want to call it. But the attitude of the generation of Migdal Bavel was "*pen nafutz*—lest we disperse," which is what they did not want to happen. Immediately after that, the next character by the name of Avraham Avinu is told "*lech*," meaning "walk and disperse." He is then told, "ונברכו בך כל משפחת האדמה—And all the families of the earth shall bless themselves by you," which can be explained as: Do not limit yourself to one area, to one zone, to one place.[2] Instead, walk and walk and walk. In this contrast, we can see that there's an idea of a lifestyle of mediocracy that is scared of growth. You did not need to grow in the generation of Migdal Bavel; the attitude was that you just needed to build together and everything would be calm, sufficient, and good. In contrast, the idea of Avraham Avinu was to realize that wherever there is struggle, there is also growth. The struggle of Avraham is that he arrived in the land thinking he'd have a child, but then he didn't have a child; thinking he'd see Hashem, but then he didn't see Hashem; thinking he'd have food, but then he didn't have food. However, Avraham understood that the *halichah*, the journey, is all about understanding that struggle is not a problem. Instead, struggle is the opportunity to develop one's character.

A second understanding of the importance of the word *lech* to define Avraham can be learned from the fact that his story opens up with the words "*lech lecha*," meaning, you have to walk. But in the next parashah, *Parashat Vayeira*, it says, "ולך לך אל ארץ המריה."[3] Avraham Avinu walks

---

1   *Bereishit* 11:4.

2   *Bereishit* 12:3.

3   *Bereishit* 22:2.

     Important to note that these are the only two times the phrase לך לך appears in the entire Torah: at the beginning and at the end of Avraham's story.

from the beginning, but he keeps walking in the end too. His story is not about walking to one destination, but rather the destination is the walking. There are two ways to growth. One way you see a result. This means that I need to get a degree from university. So why do I go to high school? I go to high school because I'm walking *toward* university. The idea of this type of *halichah* is that I am going to fight, and I am going to struggle because there will be a result.

With Avraham Avinu, he walks at the beginning and walks at the end, and therefore, says the *Sefat Emet*, the definition of Avraham Avinu is walking—not as to get to a result, but to walk because it changes who you are.

How does walking change who you are? It means that Avraham Avinu realized that walking was really about being independent. Avraham Avinu's nature was not to find solutions from someone. Wherever he had a problem, Avraham did not ask someone else for a solution. He understood that *halichah* means being independent. To be independent means that I do not want other people to solve the problems in my life. Yes, there are minor problems like: What do I need for breakfast. That is something you can ask someone to help you out with. But with something that defines your *character*, you cannot let someone else solve the problem.

I saw a video yesterday from my *rebbi*, Reb Aron Blumenfeld, and it showed a video of people walking while using their cellphones. The people in the video were completely immersed and very involved. They walked into ponds, and they fell down. They walked into other people and crashed. They walked on steps, and they fell down.

Avraham Avinu's core was *halichah* in order to build. The *Sefat Emet* gives over a profound idea. The *nisyonot*, tests, of Avraham were centered around one concept: *yelech b'atzmo*. The core of Avraham's identity was *lech lecha*, and the idea of the *nisayon* is not to wait for someone to give you an opportunity to solve it, but to understand that the core idea of your personality is *she'yelech b'atzmo*.

This week is the yahrzeit of *Moreinu v'Rabbeinu*, Rav Kalonymus Kalman Shapira, the Piaseczna Rebbe, who has walked with me my entire life since tenth grade. One of the reasons that I connect with him is because of one story. I was in tenth grade and my *rebbi* told me a story about the Piaseczna Rebbe when he was in the Warsaw Ghetto. He heard a rumor that there was a woman who had just given birth to a child. Her husband was taken days before the birth. So, this woman needed to perform a brit in the ghetto on her own. After the Rebbe heard of this child being born, he counted seven days. On the eighth day after *vatikin*, the early morning prayers, he walked outside a far distance in the snow to perform the *brit milah* for the child of this woman.

I remember that when I heard this story, I got so angry. I said that this didn't make any sense to me. Halachically, this was *pikuach nefesh*, not just because it was cold outside or because he probably didn't have shoes, but he could have gotten killed for doing this. He didn't need to do it; it wasn't even a mitzvah. My *rebbi* then told me something very sharp: If you are looking in the world of results, he was halachically exempt from doing this. But what he felt was that following the laws of Judaism wasn't always easy, and by him walking to give this boy a *brit milah*, he was defining the concept of enjoying the action of trying, because it is not only about the results but enjoying the journey of trying to keep the mitzvot.

We can learn from both the character of the Piaseczna Rebbe and Avraham Avinu that trying is greater than succeeding. The idea of Avraham is that he walked and sometimes did not succeed, and that was his ability. That was what made him unique. That he was not there for success, he was there to try.

My berachah as we enter into *Parashat Lech Lecha* and into the character of Avraham Avinu, together with the idea in the story of the Piaseczna Rebbe, is that we should all realize that all of Avraham's *nisyonot* were really one.

Lech lecha means try. You might not solve everything. You might not always be able to have the right answer on how to educate your children. You might not always know the right option for a student who walks into your office about what they should do. You might not always know what's the right way to get your children to love Hashem. But the goal is to let go of succeeding and to realize that *lech lecha* is not in order to get to "X" but it's in order to walk for the sake of walking because that means you're trying. Trying means that you care, and if you care it means that you will enjoy the mitzvot you do.

LIVING THE LEARNING

Try to walk every day for five minutes without a destination. Just let the walking define you; it may surprise you.

Parashat Lech Lecha

LETTING GO WILL BUILD YOU STRONGER

WE ARE ENTERING into the story of our nation. We enter through a character by the name of Avraham Avinu, and there are about fifty-thousand books written about Avraham, so we are just going to focus on one simple question: What made Avraham the founder of Am Yisrael?

There are obviously so many answers, but one of them is linked to the big question of why do most of us not succeed in fulfilling our dreams? There is no one in this world who doesn't have a dream. A dream could be for happiness, success, or for many different things, but so often we meet failure more than we meet success. The simple question is, why don't we succeed? Avraham was able to! Avraham had a vision—a vision which still lives on today in Yerushalayim—when he was far out near Iraq's borders. What did Avraham do right in order to succeed in his dream? The answer is connected to something interesting in the first *pasuk* about Avraham Avinu. The *pasuk* says, "ויאמר י-הוה אל אברם לך לך מארצך וממולדתך ומבית אביך אל הארץ אשר אראך—God said to Avram, 'Go forth from your native land and from your father's house to the land that I will show you.'"[1] What does the prefix, mem "mei" mean? It is translated as the word "from." Hashem said, "You have a vision Avraham; you want to go to the land. You want to not only get there, but you want to stay there. You don't only want to stay there, but you want to make it become a story that will last for thousands of years. It starts from realizing that how you are going to get there is not the number one question. Instead, the number one question is realizing what you

---

1   *Bereishit* 12:1.

23

are leaving. You cannot build something new if you are attached to something old. You cannot become a founder if you're still connected to things that are preventing you from the vision you have."

The number one answer for Avraham Avinu of what made him fitting to be the founder of our nation is that he realized that all the lofty goals, all the big visions, all the great characters and books written throughout our history all started from the same questions of, "What is preventing the dream from being realized? What is limiting me from getting there? What is holding me back and what is stopping me?"

I think that is the number one question that Am Yisrael has to realize through Avraham Avinu's character, which is that Avraham started from a story that didn't jump. We are all jumpers. We like to jump to the endzone. We jump to where we want to go. We jump to the result, but we are not willing to ask the deeper question: Why am I not there yet? There's something else holding me back, holding me down, and preventing me. For 1,948 years before Avraham Avinu was born, we had the generation of Migdal Bavel who had a great vision. They wanted to unite the world, build things, and have an identity. But it all came crashing down. The reason is because they never asked the first question of "What is preventing the world from being caring?"

I know that you want big things, but what really comes down to wanting big things is the ability to ask the letter *mem*, "*mei*." What are you willing to let go of? What is holding you back? What is preventing you? That is sometimes even more important than trying to get to the endzone.

Parashat Vayeira

REVEALING THE LIGHT

*Rav Yair talks about how the brit milah represents
the revealing of the goodness that is in each person.*

> "Most of the times the greatest treasures are not
> across oceans; they are right under your pillow."

OPENING QUESTIONS

1. Why is the *brit milah* the first mitzvah of a newborn boy?
2. Why is the act of *brit milah* so transformative with the narrative of Avraham Avinu?
3. Why is Avraham renamed just by adding a "*hei*" in the middle of his name?
4. Can you think of a link between the fact that Hashem's first action in the world was "להבדיל בין האור ובין החושך—to separate light from darkness,"[1] and the first action of a Jew is *brit milah* ?

LEARNING CONVERSATION

When we look at the end of *Parashat Lech Lecha*, we see it finishes with the *brit milah* of Avraham Avinu, and immediately after that it says, "וירא אליו ה׳—Hashem appeared to him."[2]

Two unique things happen as a result of the *brit milah*. First, immediately after the *brit milah*, Avraham Avinu's name is changed from Avram

---

1   *Bereishit* 1:18.
2   *Bereishit* 18:1.

to Avraham. With everything else he did, his name wasn't changed. He made aliyah, and his name wasn't changed. He was able to separate from Lot and fight a world war, but his name wasn't changed. He did a *brit milah*, and suddenly his identity was transformed. So obviously, the first question is going to be: Why did the *brit milah* specifically give Avraham that present or ability for the name change?

The second question: For ninety-nine years, Avraham Avinu was waiting for a child and immediately after the *brit milah*, Hashem said Sarah was going to have a child. Why was the *brit milah* what enabled Avraham to have a child with Sarah?

In order to understand the brit, the *Sefat Emet* brings a Midrash that says like this: "סוד ה' ליראיו—The secret of Hashem is with those who fear Him."[3] This *pasuk* says that the secret of Hashem is only revealed to people who have the awe of Hashem. What is the secret of Hashem? Is the secret of Hashem Shabbat? Is the secret of Hashem something where we speak about *kibbud horim*? The Midrash says one word on what the secret of Hashem is: *k'she'timol*, to be circumcised. The *brit milah* is the secret of God. Why is this considered the secret of Hashem? The *Sefat Emet* explains something transformative. He says, let's go back to the first act of Hashem: "ויבדל אלקים בין האור ובין החושך—to separate light from darkness."[4] Hashem's first act was to divide between light and darkness. The first action of Hashem allows us to understand the difference between light and darkness. The essence is *ohr*. The core is good, it's just covered by *choshech*. Our responsibility is *l'havdil bein ohr u'bein choshech*, and immediately you will see that there is *ohr*, light. The *Sefat Emet* explains that you have to understand that not only is Hashem's first act to divide between *ohr* and *choshech*, but man's first act is *brit milah*. The action of *brit milah* is *l'havdil bein ohr u'bein choshech*, to divide between something that's covering and the essence. You might have thought that in order to become a Jew, Avraham Avinu would have needed to add something: He needs to make aliyah; he needs to do all these different things; he needs to write a *Sefer Torah*; he needs to add

---

3   *Tehillim* 25:14.

4   *Bereishit* 1:4.

and add and add and add. But Hashem says no! What is going to change you and what is going to define your name is the act of *milah*, because the *brit milah* means that you take something away and you realize that Hashem was always there. It's not that you had to find someone, and you don't have to find something. You don't have to look for inspiration or something outward that's going to give you the ability. It was always there; it's just that it was covered. Therefore, the idea of *brit milah* is that it's redefining all of Judaism. It's saying that the definition of Judaism is that you have to understand what the essence is and what is covering the essence. What is covering the essence, is what we need to remove. Immediately once you subtract that, and once you remove that, you then reveal that inside you were always connected. We don't need to find answers outward because they are right there. It's just that if we live a lifestyle where we are always exposed and addicted to things that are covered, then we won't be able to see what's really there.

The *Sefat Emet* makes a very strong linguistic link between Hashem's first act and man's first action. *Ohr*, light, is composed of the letters *aleph, vav, reish*. What Hashem does is He divides the *choshech* from light. There is a second word that sounds the same and has just one letter switched which means skin, *or*, which is composed of the letters *ayin, vav, reish*. The idea of *ohr* with regard to *milah* is that we can take away the *ohr*, skin, to reveal that the inside is *ohr*. The job of the *brit milah* is for Avraham Avinu to understand that his job is not to add something new. His sole purpose is to remember something old. It's not about adding something that isn't there; it's about living out what there is with full awareness. Similar to the act of the brit, we can realize that Hashem, who is inside of us, gave us the ability to find Him.

By understanding this, we can more fully understand the significance of the change in Avraham Avinu's name. It changes from Avram to Avraham, but you might have thought that Hashem would change his whole name and his whole identity from Avram to a completely different name. But what did Hashem do after the *brit milah*? He had him keep the same name, but He just added the *hei* on the inside. The change of Avraham Avinu's name is a manifestation of the idea of taking away a cover to understand that you were *always* Avraham; it's just that you were exposed to something else, controlled by a different culture. All we have to do is take away what is preventing the light. One just needs to see what is inside, and the diamond hiding behind every locked box—to truly live like Avraham Avinu.

The berachah as we enter into this Shabbat is to understand that the job of Am Yisrael and the mission of our lives is not to try and create something new but to find something that was always there. We need to educate our children and ourselves not to think of what lies outward, but to realize that we have to understand that all we have to do is just not cover our eyes, and then we'll see that the *hei* (ה) was always there, and that Hashem was always there, and the *l'havdil bein ohr u'bein choshech* means removing the darkness and realizing that that is the only thing you need to do to find the light.

LIVING THE LEARNING

Make sure once a week to peel a vegetable to internalize the difference between what is real and what is seen.

TRY. TO TRY. TO TRY AGAIN.

THE GEMARA in *Berachot* 26b teaches us that each one of the Avot established a different *tefillah*. Avraham Avinu established *Shacharit*, Yitzchak established *Minchah*, and Yaakov established *Maariv*. The Gemara brings down different *pesukim* to teach how each of them established a *tefillah*. In our parashah, *Vayeira*, we find the *pasuk* that establishes *Shacharit* which was composed by Avraham Avinu. The *pasuk* says, "וישכם אברהם בבקר אל המקום אשר עמד שם את פני י-הוה—Avraham woke up early in the morning and hurried to the place where he had stood before the God."[1] What comes next is very, very transformative. Avraham Avinu wakes up early in the morning and what is he excited to see? He is excited to see the outcome of his *tefillah*. He wanted to see the result of his *tefillah*. So, he woke up early in the morning and went to the place where he had davened to Hashem to save Lot from destruction in order to see what happened.

The next *pasuk* is astonishing as it says, "וישקף על פני סדם ועמרה ועל כל פני ארץ הככר וירא והנה עלה קיטר הארץ כקיטר הכבשן—And, looking down toward Sodom and Gomorrah and all the land of the plain, he saw the smoke of the land rising like the smoke of a kiln."[2] What we may not realize is that we never again see Avraham and Lot together. We could read this in a way to mean that Avraham may have not even known that Lot was saved. He woke up in the morning, looked at Sodom and it was completely burnt, and we never see Avraham and Lot meet again. If we look deeper, this could mean that maybe Avraham rose up and thought

---

1   *Bereishit* 19:27.
2   *Bereishit* 19:28.

that his *tefillah* didn't work! The night before, he said to Hashem, "Please save Lot!" Avraham woke up the next morning and never saw him again. What does this teach us about the *tefillah* of *Shacharit* and Avraham Avinu?

Many of us think that we open our day to see our success, but Avraham established the idea that trying is succeeding. We know this because Avraham never saw Lot again, and he didn't know that Lot survived the destruction of Sodom. All Avraham knew was that he tried. That is the way to begin a new day. Avraham's success was that he realized that real success is measured by how much you try, the amount of effort, and not the results that one has.

In the world we live in today, it is very obvious what is considered being successful, but unfortunately, our own dreams and what we want is often overlooked. The *tefillah* of *Shacharit* of Avraham Avinu is just the opposite. He didn't realize that he was successful, and he didn't even get to see Lot! But he understood that *wanting* Lot to be saved was more significant than anything else. Our only decision in life is to try and then to let go of the results.

We should all be blessed every day that when we enter into a new day and daven *Shacharit* that we adopt the mindset of Avraham Avinu. I'm going to ask for the sake of asking. I'm going to try for the sake of trying. I'm not only going to do what I do so that the outcome will be what I'm looking for. I'll learn that the effort changes me and develops me and makes me the person that I need to be.

Parashat Chayei Sarah

LIVE FOREVER

*Rav Yair talks about the limits of time and how
Sarah teaches us how to overcome it.*

> "The best way to go out is to go in."
>
> "The external stays set but is defined by internal growth."

OPENING QUESTIONS

1. What do you think made Sarah unique?
2. Do you feel that time is something that creates excitement or pressure for you?

LEARNING CONVERSATION

One of the things that I've learned and seen is that there is a very big transition between the experience of high school to the experience after. It's the difference between a feeling of clarity and a feeling of confusion. What causes the confusion is time. If we turn around an hourglass, we'll start to feel the limit and pressure, that no matter what we want, time is stronger than our will. We are controlled and minimized by the boundaries of time.

From first to twelfth grade, time isn't free—it's controlled—so everything is clear. You're told to learn, and you learn, and once in a while you mess up. It's very obvious, and it's very structured. From the moment that someone finishes that structure, there are only opportunities—so many paths and options—but time stays the same and creates so much pressure and confusion. There is a lot of will and limited time.

The moment that someone leaves the specific expectations of a system—whether school or the army—they enter a harsh reality. "I think that this tension between clarity and doubt is something that we deal with constantly, because of the aspect of time. What I mean by this is very simple. Time defines things that are greater than us. Right now, I'm thirty-four years old, and as much as I want to run a marathon, I have to understand that every single time that I chew on a chocolate bar it's going to prevent me from being able to do that, no matter what I dream of, think of, want, or daven for. There's this idea that time limits and controls your desires and dreams. We want things to change but the truth of time is that nothing's going to change, and nothing really matters. So, I think that this tension is in the puzzle of the life of Sarah.

When we look at the end of the life of Sarah it says, "ויהיו חיי שרה מאה שנה ועשרים שנה ושבע שנים שני חיי שרה—The span of Sarah's life came to one hundred and twenty and seven years."[1] Obviously, the focus of the *pasuk* is the word *shanah*, year, which is a measure of time. We have to understand that there's something about the death of Sarah that focuses on the limits. Sarah experienced for ninety years, that no matter what she wanted, time defined her. On a certain level, she laughed when someone said to her, "Sarah will have a child." She responded "No, because I am in the realm of time, and time defines me. So, if time defines me, I will never have a child." Then comes the death of Sarah and the focus is on this word *shanah* which means days will come and days will go.

Sefer Kohelet says, "כל הנחלים הלכים אל הים והים איננו מלא—All streams flow into the sea, yet the sea is never full."[2] There's a cycle. Everything's a cycle. It's a year, and then the same circle starts again. Sarah's essence is exactly the pain of the reality of "same, same." Every day, she yearns to have a child, but the years come and go, and she is still barren.

Regarding Sarah, the Midrash gives a new perspective on her character and on time in general: "יודע ה' ימי תמימם ונחלתם לעולם תהיה—Hashem

---

1   *Bereishit* 23:1.
2   *Kohelet* 1:7.

knows the days of the righteous, and their inheritance will be forever."[3] Continues the Midrash: "כשם שהן תמימים כך שנותם תמימים."

It might sound like a simple Midrash, but really it is one of the most transformative Midrashim. It says Sarah was a person who was *tamim*—that she worked on herself, and therefore she affected time, but time did not define her. When she was a hundred years old, she was as beautiful as twenty. At twenty, it's said she was as innocent as when she was seven. The concept this Midrash is teaching is that you can live a lifestyle where time is just an opportunity, and not a limitation. If you look at Sarah's life when she was ninety, she broke the limits, and when she was a hundred, she looked like she was twenty. There is a lifestyle that causes a person not to be defined by time, but to redefine time.

What that means is something that I want to develop through the teachings of the *Sefat Emet*. The *Sefat Emet* wrote, "לכן ברא השי״ת שיהי׳ בכל יום שפע חיות מחדש."[4] There's this idea that Hashem is renewing the world all the time, but how many of us feel that? Sure, we say Hashem is renewing the world every day in davening, מחדש בטובו בכל יום תמיד—He renews daily, perpetually, the work of Creation." We say that Hashem is renewing the world, but most of us don't really think that the sun might not be there tomorrow. What we have to understand is that when you look at the world on a superficial level, everything is the same. But when you look within, you'll see that things are changing. One of the best experiences is when you try to explain to your children why not to eat seven Dunkin Donuts, and they're very, very sure that eating seven Dunkin Donuts is the best thing to do. And you say to them, "Listen, it's so unhealthy!" and the child says, "If I eat those seven Dunkin Donuts and I look in the mirror, I'm going to look the same!" On the surface, nothing changed, and even internally that's a lifestyle that will not cause you any crazy failure. It is, however, a lifestyle that if you continue with, slowly you'll become someone that is controlled, and not someone who is in control.

---

3   *Bereishit Rabbah* 58:1.
4   *Sefat Emet, Bereishit, Chayei Sarah* 4:3. Written in 1874.

In addition, the *pasuk* describes the person first, "*Vayihiyu chayei Sarah*," and then time, "*me'ah shanah*." It starts with the person, and then gives over the years. When you live a lifestyle where you begin from changing *yourself*, time is just an added ingredient to efficiency and clarity.

This can be seen through the character of Sarah. She was willing to let Hagar marry Avraham just so Avraham could have a child. She was willing to challenge herself in so many different ways: In Egypt when she was taken to the palace of Pharaoh, and when she followed Avraham and came to Israel. She challenged her personality all the time and because of that lifestyle it resulted in "*me'ah shanah v'esrim shanah*." Time changed, because she changed. Her perspective wasn't superficial any more, but rather Divine. What she did is that she realized that you have to stop looking forward, and instead look inward. What we learn about Sarah is that she's inside the *ohel*, "*v'Sarah shomaat petach ha'ohel*"[5]—and if you're inside the *ohel*, and you're changing, your perspective of the world changes.

On a linguistic level, the word *shanah* means time, but it also means *shinui*, change. It's the same root-word, and on a certain level what it's saying is that there are two lifestyles: One where you run after time, and the other where you let go of time. When you let go of time, you're saying: I'm not running after something before I know why I'm running after it. If you know why you're running, every second is going to be so different. We know that when you're clear about why you're walking into your chuppah, that second lasts forever. But the question is, Why does it feel that way? It's just one second! But you transform your perspective, your personality, and your outlook. You've built it, and now that one second isn't *shanah*, year, but its *shinui*, change.

My berachah, as we enter into the end of the life of Sarah, is that we should realize that time is not limiting. Time is inviting us to not go forward before going inward. I heard this cute sentence that I thought about this week, and it's, "Before you go out, you have to go in." We

---

5   *Bereishit* 18:10.

know that going out means going on a date or going out with someone. Everyone's talking about it, "Oh she's going out with this person," and "He's going out with that person." But you can only go out if you go in. Sarah went in, and therefore time was an opportunity. When we don't go in, time becomes scary. We should have that ability with our families this Shabbat to not look at how we run forward before we have the time to focus inward—then all time becomes a *hazmanah*, an invitation. It's not *z'man*, time, it's an invitation to decide how I, as a person, choose to enjoy my time because I have realized what I want and why I want it, and so time isn't limiting me anymore.

LIVING THE LEARNING

Don't wear a watch for a day or two…

Parashat Chayei Sarah

SARAH POWER

WHEN WE ENTER into *Parashat Chayei Sarah*, the opening *pasuk* is: "ויהיו חיי שרה מאה שנה ועשרים שנה ושבע שנים שני חיי שרה—Sarah's lifetime, the span of Sarah's life, came to one hundred and twenty-seven years."[1] Very often people realize that there is one word that is emphasized again and again. This word is *shanah*, year. This is the last *pasuk* that describes the life of Sarah. We therefore have to ask ourselves a question: Who was Sarah? Every time she appears, it is in places of extreme adversity. She appears going down to Egypt; not knowing if she will live. She appears for the first time when being introduced as *"eshet Avram, Sarai."* She is a woman that is introduced through adversity. She had a child. This child was being influenced and affected by Yishmael. Then the child was almost taken away from her. There are no stories with Sarah that are calm, relaxed, or normal. She is introduced constantly with challenges and difficulties. What does the last *pasuk* teach us about Sarah? It teaches us the word of *shanah*. In 1871, the *Sefat Emet* asked what this repeating of the word *shanah* signified. He answered that for most people, time changes them. Reality affects them. Sadness affects them. In a place of happiness, they become happy, and in a place of adversity, they are gone and finished. The *Sefat Emet* says that the last idea of Sarah is the word *shanah*. She was consistently affected by external factors, but it only changed her externally. She was not affected internally. Sarah was able to see a world that took everything from her, and it did not change her. "מאה שנה ועשרים שנה ושבע שנים" means that Sarah could be

---

1   *Bereishit* 23:1.

36

someone who physical reality had no effect on. But what does it mean that reality has no effect, when obviously it does affect us? It really means that Sarah believed that man is not controlled. Things will hurt us, things might be challenging for us, but we are the ones who decide what goes in. With everything that Sarah went though, nothing went in. Inside there was only one thing. Inside, Sarah knew that the future is something that we never let go of. If we have a vision of our future, the present is just an opportunity. If we have vision, everything we see is an opportunity. To understand this on a deeper level, the first halachah in the *Shulchan Aruch* is about waking up for *vatikin*. The halachah says "שיהא הוא מעורר השחר"—that a person should awaken the sun."[2] But all of us know we cannot awaken the sun—it rises by itself! The halachah says that, yes, you cannot externally control the sun, but internally, if you have such a demand for your future and you wake up before the sun, then it could be possible to raise up the world. The present—if we have vision—is something we can utilize, something we can affect.

My berachah going into the last moments of Sarah's life is to realize that Sarah said we all have to make a decision. Are we external people, and therefore we are always defined? Or are we internal people, and we always define others? This is the message of Sarah: because she was internally aware, nothing externally was hurting her. With that we should walk into a Shabbat, when so many thousands of members of Am Yisrael are going to Chevron, we should realize that the message of Sarah is that we need to have vision. Then we can enjoy the challenges of the world. But if we lose vision, then the challenges of the world will always control us, and we will not control them.

---

2   *Shulchan Aruch, Orach Chayim* 1:1.

Parashat Toldot

CONSISTENCY

Yitzchak is the father of consistency.

"What makes a seed into a tree is someone who is willing
to boringly pour water on it every single day."

OPENING QUESTIONS

1. What makes Yitzchak different than Avraham and Yaakov? How do these differences draw the identity of Yitzchak's character?
2. Yitzchak has one main story just for him: the digging of the wells. What do you make of this?

LEARNING CONVERSATION:

Parashat Toldot is a unique parashah that deals with a difficult character. This character is one that we don't have many books about. If anyone thinks about Avraham Avinu and walks into any library, there will be hundreds and hundreds of books. If you write a story about Yaakov Avinu, you'll see movies and books. However, when it comes to Yitzchak, we just skip it and go on to the next parashah. But if there is a parashah that deals with the character of Yitzchak, it is *Parashat Toldot*.

The character of Yitzchak can be understood through one story since there is only one story that is solely about Yitzchak. It's the story of Yitzchak digging three wells, and it's only fifteen *pesukim*! He re-digs the wells that Avraham, his father, dug, and then there was a fight over it so he called it Esek. Then he dug again, and there was another fight, and Yitzchak called it Sitnah. He dug again, and there was not a fight, so he called it Rechovot. Obviously, everyone is sitting around asking themselves, "Ribbono Shel Olam, is this the only thing you have to tell us about Yitzchak? There are many better stories and great stories that You could tell us about Yitzchak, but You decided to focus on digging wells. What is so significant about this?" Obviously, we know the answer is that this is not all about digging wells. It is that the concept of digging wells is a symbol of what Yitzchak's identity was all about.

The *Sefat Emet* wrote, אא״ז מו״ר זצלל״ה הגיד בענין הבארות שהם להסיר החיצוניות והסתר למצוא הנקודה.[1] The *Sefat Emet* explains that you have to realize that when you're digging a well, you have to work very hard. You work so hard until you reveal that there is something underneath the surface called water. That water is something that was always there; it just was secretly waiting for you to toil to dig for it. The action of digging the well requires that you have the patience and the consistency to be willing to work day and night, just to reveal the water that you know is hidden below. The action of digging a well, more than the water itself, shows the consistency and determination to work through all the things that are covering it. Connecting to the essence of life is not only achieved through *chiddushim*, realizations. Often, we think that in order to reveal Hashem we have to have a new book. You walk into a library, and you see that everybody has new *sefarim*. If we think about the identity of Avraham Avinu, every single parashah has a new story and a great story, and therefore it's focused on *chiddushim*. But the character of Yitzchak was to dig. To understand that as great as realizations, revelations, and even a first date are, what's much more special than a great date is the ability to know that you are willing to walk patiently through the intricacies of life. What creates greatness isn't knowing that you can create something new but that you can continue something old.

I think that what the *Sefat Emet* is saying is that the action of Yitzchak is digging wells. The character of Yitzchak is that he never left the land, which is different from Avraham and Yaakov. Both Avraham and Yaakov

---

1   *Sefat Emet, Bereishit, Toldot* 1:3. Written in 1871.

had their names changed, but Yitzchak's name was never changed. Avraham had two wives, and Yaakov had four wives, but Yitzchak had only one. The idea of Yitzchak is very important. He believed that in order to affect the future and in order to find the water that would revive the world, he needed to have the patience to be consistent and dig.

When you work on consistency, you understand that it's not about learning a new idea, but it's about a lifestyle of determination and hard work. I think that this connects to one more thing mentioned in the parashah: When Yitzchak wanted to give the berachah to Eisav, he said to him one thing that makes no sense. He said to him, "Eisav, you want the berachah? All you have to do is go find me a piece of steak in the field." Everyone looks at this and says, what in the world does this have to do with receiving the berachah? If you want to give the berachah, then give the berachah. You don't want to give the berachah, then don't give the berachah. The idea that Yitzchak was saying to Eisav was, you have to understand that the berachah is not the main point, but rather the journey to the berachah is the reason for the berachah. The journey of the berachah is to go out into the field, to a world of consistent work, and *only then* can you earn the berachah.

We should all have the berachah to realize that it's not all about the smile, but it's about the willingness to sit through what is boring, to be determined and consistent. Only then can you really realize that you'll find the water that will sustain life—not water that will become something that you need someone to give you, but something that you earn because you were willing to patiently search for it on a daily basis. This is one of the greatest characteristics of Yitzchak.

LIVING THE LEARNING

Make a coffee for someone you don't have the greatest connection to for the next thirty days.

YITZCHAK DIGS IN

THIS PARASHAH deals with Yitzchak Avinu, and there are a lot of ways to differentiate between Avraham and Yitzchak. One of the ways we can tell them apart is by looking at the difference between mountains and wells. The last story of Avraham Avinu's life is in *Bereishit* 22, the story of the *Akeidah*. There we see that Avraham says "בהר י-הוה יראה—Hashem will be seen in the mountain." In a certain way, Avraham was saying that the idea of his life was about mountains; that you have to go higher, and even if you think you have climbed enough, you have to climb more. Even if you think there is something that stopped, you have to build more. You have to reveal and build; this is the image of Avraham Avinu. When we go into *Parashat Toldot*, we see Yitzchak doing a different action; he digs wells. Yitzchak puts a lot of emphasis on them, the names he calls them, and the actions he was performing. We can see that Yitzchak was not about the mountain, but rather he was about the well. What does it mean that Yitzchak is so different, that he does not build and climb mountains, but rather that he digs wells? On a certain level when you dig a well, no one else cares; it is unseen, and only you know where it is. In contrast, with a mountain, everyone looks at it and sees it.

Yitzchak is someone who understands that as much as Avraham was transforming the outside, by influencing others, giving, and doing, there was still something that was missing in the world. There was a need for someone to be able to go down, dig deeper, know how to be alone, and to know that even if they were only fixing themselves, they were an image of the world. When you are digging a well and no one else can see it, this does not mean it does not matter. We often think that

41

what people do not see is irrelevant. Yitzchak says the opposite: what people do not see is the most relevant.

My berachah, as we enter into *Parashat Toldot* and we look into Yitzchak, is that we should realize that as we do so many things in the world and have many things going on, the people that really matter are the ones that know what we do—when no one else really knows what is going on. It is all about the relationships that you don't show to the outside world, and the home you are building inside. If you have an inner vision, a dream, and a perspective of what you want to accomplish, you should be *zocheh* to realize and build the wells of Yitzchak. With that we can then build back the mountain of Har HaMoriah.

Parashat Vayetzei

HAVE A ROPE

Rav Yair discusses the special term "vayetzei,"
and the lessons we can learn from it.

> "The mindset you have is more relevant than reality."
>
> "Perception can't change a situation, but it does
> define the result or impact of a situation."
>
> "You can go so low if you are aware of
> how low you are descending."

OPENING QUESTIONS

1. Why do you think Yaakov went to Charan?
2. How is it that with all the ordeals of Charan and Lavan that not only did Yaakov keep 613 mitzvot, but he thrived and found his wives and children?
3. When is it possible to excel in uninspiring and difficult realities? And when is it too dangerous to enter negative and uninspiring atmospheres?

LEARNING CONVERSATION

I want to focus on one *pasuk* from the parashah. The opening *pasuk* of this parashah says, "ויצא יעקב מבאר שבע וילך חרנה."[1] The translation is simply that Yaakov left from Be'er Sheva and went to Charan. On the superficial level, this *pasuk* describes a journey. But a few things

---

1   *Bereishit* 28:10.

make this *pasuk* a very strong guide for life. Why are the places so important, and why do these two places need to be emphasized? If the context of this *pasuk* is that Yaakov is fleeing from a scary brother who clearly wanted to kill him, then the opening word should have been "*vayivrach*," and he ran away from Eisav, not the word choice "*vayetzei*,"?

According to the teachings of *Chassidut*, the story is dealing with how someone enters into a place they know is difficult. How do you enter into Charan? How do you enter somewhere you have no father or mother, no *beit midrash*, or no land? Yaakov already had a great life. He lived in Chevron and in Be'er Sheva, and he had his parents there. He had the *bechorah* and then got the berachah from his father Yitzchak. Suddenly, he had to leave this ideal life and had nothing left. The *pasuk* is dealing with the question of how we should approach entering stages in life that aren't simple. As we mentioned before, there are two things that stand out about the *pasuk*: The first is that it says *vayetzei* and not *vayivrach*. The second interesting thing to note is that there is a focus on the places, as it says: "Yaakov left Be'er Sheva and set out for Charan."

An interesting point that could be learned from the choice of *vayetzei*, leaving, and not *vayivrach*, fleeing, is the fact that he really was running away. The idea here is that in reality the situation was difficult, but the perception is up to the person. You can decide if you are a result of reality or if you feel that even though reality is saying "X" that you are willing to think differently. Even though nature says to think one way or act in a certain manner, a person always can try and define their nature. Maybe Yaakov was saying, *vayetzei*, that in reality, he was running away, but due to his mindset, he would never let himself go anywhere out of the feeling of being forced. The idea of *vayetzei* is that even though things may be difficult in reality, your mindset is your own, and you must decide what that is going to be. The mindset of Yaakov was that he would never do something that he didn't decide to do or choose to do. Yes, the reality might not be able to be changed, but our mindset is something that we can be in control of. Our mindset is something that no one can control for us.

The *Zohar Hakadosh*, in describing Yaakov's journey down to Charan, writes, "מי שרוצה לירד לבור."[2] The emphasis is on the word *rotzeh*, that a person *wants* to go into a difficult situation. The fact that a person begins from the perspective of wanting means that the pit can become much more than face value. The experience of Charan was a *bor*, a pit, and Yaakov wanted and decided to enter into this dark and unknown place. The *Zohar* is teaching that more important than where you are going is how you are going—the perspective you have and the atmosphere you bring with you into the new reality. Through Yaakov, we can learn that you can overcome Charan. You can overcome all the obstacles. But there is a condition: you have a rope. If you do not have an mindset or a lifestyle that you can hold onto, then you are not entering the pit from strength, and you won't truly able to make an effect.

The idea is that he was leaving from Be'er Sheva, because that is his *chevel chazak*, strong rope, meaning that he understood exactly what he was doing. All of us ask about the Lubavitcher Rebbe: How could it be that all of his students are all over the world and still love Shabbat? They are in the middle of Afghanistan and very distant places. Then you look at the communities that we live in like Toronto, in Montreal, in Hollywood, Florida, or in the middle of New York, which are surrounded by every opportunity and have every great kosher restaurant you could ask for, yet no one is connected. So, what happened? How could this be that so many kids are struggling to connect, in places that have so much opportunity, yet the *shluchim* of the Rebbe are in desolate places where all they have is themselves, and they are thriving? The answer could be simple. When you know that you have a *chevel*, rope, you are always making an impact. But when you lose that rope, you are falling, and falling, and falling with no way to get out.

How do we enter Charan? The answer is, we need two things. Firstly, we need to know that our mindset is more than what we think. The mindset that we enter with will completely change the experience. For Yaakov, it was either *vayetzei* or *vayivrach*, but because he left out of

---

2   *Sefat Emet, Bereishit, Vayetzei* 3.

choice, he was able to overcome—and he also got married and had his children there—all because he was able to change his mindset. Changing our mindset may not change the struggle, but it will change the *result* of the struggle. The second thing is to not enter into a reality of struggle if you don't have a rope. If you don't have something strong that you are committed to—something strong that you are coming from—then you are going to fall apart when you enter into the new reality.

LIVING THE LEARNING

Buy a rope—and put a sticker on it with who or what your rope is.

Parashat Vayetzei

CHOOSING TO CHANGE

GOING BACK to the end of last parashah, we find a very interesting topic. We know that Eisav despised his brother Yaakov, to the extent that Yaakov had to leave and go into exile. If we look at the description of Rivkah, she said that he should leave Israel as a runaway. Like we know from *The Lion King*, the *chevrah* come to Simba and they say, "Run away, and never return." They learned it from Rivkah. She said to Yitzchak, "Tell our child to run away until Eisav calms down." Yet when Yitzchak sent Yaakov, he gave a totally different reason from what Rivkah told him to say. He said, "Go find a wife. Go to Charan, and find a wife." Two totally different reasons! One negative and one positive. In our parashah, it gets even more complicated because the description was to run away, but the *pasuk* starts and says *vayeitzei*, go out.

The *Sefat Emet* notes this choice of word of *vayeitzei*, go out, should have been *vayivrach*, run away. *Vayivrach* implies a necessity, meaning that he needed to run, whereas *vayeitzei* implies that there was choice. We don't even know why he left, as it says, "ויצא יעקב מבאר שבע וילך חרנה—Yaakov left Be'er Sheva and set out for Haran."[1] It doesn't give Yitzchak's reason. It doesn't give Rivkah's reason. It doesn't say *vayivrach*. It says *vayeitzei*. So, the question is, what is the story of Yaakov? It doesn't describe that he's going because he's looking for a wife, and it doesn't seem like he's afraid of Eisav. Here, Yaakov is saying something very new. He's saying, the only way to survive is to thrive. The

---

1   *Bereishit* 28:10.

only way to overcome is to have vision. The only way to excel is to see things beyond.

On a superficial level it's true that Yaakov was running away from Eisav, and it's also true that he was searching for a wife, but Yaakov says if you're living on a superficial level, you will never win. Anyone that can't create an addition, something new, will end up becoming irrelevant. If the mitzvot we do are the mitzvot that were given to us, and we don't add an element or layer to them, then we will end up resenting the mitzvot that we do. If our davening at the age of six is the way that we daven at the age of sixty, then you have never grown in your davening. We all know the Mishnah, "רבי אליעזר אומר, העושה תפלתו קבע, אין תפלתו תחנונים—Rabbi Eliezer says: One whose prayer is fixed, his prayer is not supplication and is flawed."[2] If you make your *tefillah* without layers and without additions, then it means you don't truly understand the idea of relationships. It can't be something that's stale; it needs to be refreshed.

So, Yaakov made a statement by saying, *vayeitzei*. I know what my *abba* said, and I know what my *imma* said. I will listen, but now I am going to make it my own. I'm going to go out of my own choice. Yaakov made a decision that he needed to add. If we are adding, then we are going to get excited. If we are following, then we are going to get bored.

We are entering into Chanukah, and we know that Beit Hillel teaches us that the idea of the candles is to add each night. He is saying here that adding is the definition of growth. If you want to grow and change, then you need to start adding and give more layers to the cake.

My berachah as we enter into the story of Yaakov Avinu is that, living in a world that the highest level that people sometimes reach is complaining, maybe we could replace the complaining with adding, and instead of complaining that "this isn't the way I wanted it," we chose to add something. The void will then no longer be a void because it will become something that enables you to feel that you are relevant and building. We can then all become like Yaakov Avinu.

---

2   *Berachot* 4:4.

Parashat Vayishlach

SUNRISE

"Growth is not growing up, it is growing forward! This is also known as the ability to converse directly with our struggles."

OPENING QUESTIONS

1. Yaakov's two names are Yaakov and Yisrael. What do you think the differences between the two names are, and what do they teach us about Yaakov?
2. What makes a person independent—someone who can lead themselves and others on their own, without being dependent on others to lead them?
3. Yaakov's name was changed after he fought with the angel. What was it about this act that was strong enough to cause Yaakov to get a name change?

LEARNING CONVERSATION

This parashah brings us to a very important moment. Yaakov Avinu gets the moment he has been waiting for and his name is changed. His first and second name are a reflection of the deep internal journey that Yaakov goes through in his life.

His first name was Yaakov, and there's two things we must focus on regarding his first name. The first is that he was holding onto the heel of someone else, meaning the name of Yaakov signifies that he didn't really have a name. He had a name of holding onto someone else which means that he was passive and dependent on Eisav. The second part is physically, the *eikev* is the heel, which is the lowest part of the body. Yaakov started from a place of dependency and the lowest part, but his second name was very different. His second name was Yisrael, as it says, "כי שרית עם אלוקים ועם אנשים ותוכל—For you have striven with beings, divine and human, and have prevailed."[1] The name Yisrael can be divided into two: *Yashar E-l*. This can be translated as "directly to Hashem." In other words, Yaakov transitioned from the lowest to the highest. The second part of the name change shows that he has his own action, "*ki sarita*—because you fought." We can see that there is a big transition between the first and second names. The first is the heel, and the second is that you are going straight to Hashem. The first is that you are linked with and dependent on someone else, and here it's your own action. The question is simply, what happened at the moment that Yaakov's name changed that allowed him to transition from Lifestyle A to Lifestyle B?

The *Sefat Emet* said something incredible that can really help us understand what happened at that moment.[2] He said that the name of Yisrael and the identity of the Jewish people are connected to the fact that we fought. So, the question of what it means that Yaakov fought against the angel is answered by the *Sefat Emet*. If we look at the action that took place in the parashah, it was in the middle of the night, pitch dark, and nobody was with Yaakov. After finding his four wives, his children, and all his possessions, he was left with nothing; it was all gone. The *pasuk* says, "ויותר יעקב לבדו ויאבק איש עמו—Yaakov was left alone, and a figure wrestled with him."[3] This means that he was all alone, and someone was fighting him. You would think that this would be something negative, but the *Zohar Hakadosh* says: No! The angel that was fighting with Yaakov was the angel that was protecting him. As it says, "מלאכיו יצוה לך לשמרך—He will order His angels to guard you."[4] How could it be that someone who is punching you and confronting

---

1   *Bereishit* 32:29.
2   In the year 1873.
3   *Bereishit* 32:25.
4   *Sefat Emet, Bereishit, Vayishlach* 3:3.

you could also be protecting you? Explains the *Zohar:* Through our two *yetzarim, yetzer hatov* and *yetzer hara.*[5] Often we convince ourselves that the *yetzer hara* is bad and negative, but we forget the first word, *yetzer,* means desire. *Yetzer* is the word of Creation and the *ra* is there to enable us to create. The best present or angel is not the one that is telling us that everything is good, that we are perfect, or that we get a gold medal for being last place, but rather, it's the one that is confronting us and believing in us enough to demand of us!

For Yaakov's entire life, he was running away from problems. Every time there was a problem, he solved it by doing something else. One wife didn't work out, so he got another one. He didn't get the *bechorah,* so he looked for the *bechorah.* Yet, he never confronted Eisav. He never stood face to face with him and said "You know what? The fact that I am struggling is good!" We can see this in any real relationship. The closer you get to someone, the more you fight with them. When you fight with people you are not close to you just run away, but when you fight with people you really care about, you stay with them anyway. The moment Yaakov's life changes is when he realizes that confronting Eisav is the only real solution. That standing and struggling with Eisav is confronting the negative, and standing face to face with the darkness and not running away from it is really the solution of how to transition from a dependent person into an independent person.

Just to end off, I think that we speak to our generation about being inspired to love Hashem and all these great ideas, but the struggle of running away and not addressing reality stems from something much deeper. Our true struggle is because we're not solving anything. We are not willing to address the difficulties that we have. We don't want to address the reality—that we are addicted to being dependent on the world. If we are not able to confront that, then our names will never change. Too often, we are solving things by creating an image of something else, but really our job is to enter and *le'abek,* to confront. Only if we are willing to have the real conversations with our children, the real

---

5   *Zohar* 1:201a:9.

conversations with our friends and with our wives, then this confrontation is what will protect us, not hurt us.

The berachah, as we see the name change of Yaakov, is to also change our lifestyles, from lifestyles that create external solutions by making everything look good, to creating an internal solution where we are willing and excited to struggle with the world of Eisav.

LIVING THE LEARNING

Stand in front of a mirror on Erev Shabbat and speak to yourself about the areas in your character that you think are pulling you down.

Parashat Vayishlach / Chanukah

WEAK SIDE, STRONG SIDE

IN PARASHAT VAYISHLACH we are introduced to the birth of the last tribe of Am Yisrael, Binyamin. We know that Binyamin received two names. When he is born in this parashah, his *imma* realized that it was near the end of her life: "ויהי בצאת נפשה כי מתה ותקרא שמו בן אוני ואביו קרא לו בנימין—But as she breathed her last, for she was dying, she named him Ben-oni; but his father called him Binyamin."[1] And *oni* is from the word "poverty" meaning pain, meaning Binyamin was the "child of pain." He was the child of difficulty and the child where Rachel left the world. However, his father Yaakov called him Binyamin which is the exact opposite and which relates to the Hebrew word *yamin* which means the right side. Binyamin was the "son of strength." We see a hidden debate here between Rachel and Yaakov about the last tribe's name. Rachel sees it for what it is: the pain and the challenge. Yaakov sees it for what it will be: the strength. The question becomes, is there a deeper conversation happening here between Rachel and Yaakov? It's possible that together, they are teaching us the secret of Chanukah.

We know that we are entering Chanukah and we want to connect this inner conversation to the secret of Chanukah. We know that in *Shirat HaYam* we say, "ימינך י-הוה נאדרי בכח ימינך י-הוה תרעץ אויב—Your right hand, God, glorious in power, Your right hand, God, shatters the foe!"[2] The word *yamin* appears twice here. The *Sefat Emet* asks why we relate to Hashem by saying *yamin* twice? We know there's always left and right, a stronger side and a weaker side. Why do we need to say *yamin*

---

1   *Bereishit* 35:18.
2   *Shemot* 15:6.

twice to relate to Hashem? The answer the *Sefat Emet* gives connects to Chanukah.

Chanukah is the only time throughout the year that we begin from the left. Firstly, we know the Chanukah candles are placed on the left side of the entrance of our home. We also light the candles from left to right. We see that we begin from the weaker side, the left which represents difficulty. The concept of Chanukah is that when you are in a relationship with Hashem the left becomes the right. The *Sefat Emet* explains that when you are away from Hashem there are differences. There is good and there is bad. There is lazy and there is productive. There is fun and there is boring. When we are living distant from Hashem, things are different. There is left and there is right. But we know that if we take the left and the right—which on their own are different—and bring them together, it creates a sound. Reb Nachman teaches that this is the secret to having a relationship with Hashem: When we realize that the differences are in truth just complimenting and assisting each other. Yes, there are things that we are not good at and things that we are good at, but in Chanukah we are realizing that the greatest relationship with Hashem is when you understand that being close to Hashem means that the differences come together. It is when the left is not alone anymore and no longer distant, but it's beginning the journey to the right side, and they are connecting to each other and they are relating to each other.

This is why, in *Shirat HaYam*, we say *yamin* twice because in our world there is imperfect and perfect. But if we were to go to the root of a tree, there is no bad and good; it's all united. In the appearance of the world there will be separations just like the tree's branches, but in the root of existence it's all connected to *yamin*, Hashem. It's all connected to direction. It's all connected to relationships.

To return to the naming of Binyamin, we see that Rachel and Yaakov were teaching us a new idea. Binyamin, in the moment of his birth, seemed to be the end. It seemed to be the last Tribe and the ending of the story. Rachel was no longer in the world, but her ending was also the beginning of *mevakah al baneha*. Binyamin, the last tribe, is also the tribe in whose territory the Beit Hamikdash would be built. It seems like he is the end because he is so alone, by himself, and the only one born in Israel. But really, he was born in Israel to show that he is the concept of connecting the end to the beginning.

At some point in our lives, we have to stop living with the feeling that we are here and we are there, and must realize that everything is interdependent. That when I wake up five minutes late, it affects the rest of my day. They are connected in a good and a bad way, but regardless, they are connected. We can't create voids, and the whole secret of Chanukah is that we should no longer be afraid of the void. We are ready to enter below the ten *tefachim* where we light the Chanukah candles. We are ready to embrace the left, the challenges, the sides that we are not sure of, because having a connection to Hashem means seeing that *oni* and *yamin* are talking to each other. That left and right are creating a clap. That the end of something is also the beginning.

The secret that we all have to bless each other upon entering Chanukah is that, yes, in the experience of the world things are divided. There are people that we are close to who we have not seen for a long time, and we can't do the things that we love. But, if we are in a relationship with our families, with our friends, and with Hashem, then even distance can become closeness.

THE LONG-TERM AFFECTER

*Rav Yair talks about Yosef as the example of
a shaliach with its benefits and dangers.*

> "The permission to affect others is dependent on the
> fact that a person knows they have been affected."

OPENING QUESTIONS

1. What are the connections or differences between Yaakov and Yosef?
2. What are the differences between Yaakov and Yosef in the way they dealt with struggles?
3. How would you define Yosef's style of life?
4. What enabled Yosef to deal with and overcome the many ordeals he went through from when he was sold by his brothers and all the obstacles after that?

LEARNING CONVERSATION

B'siyata d'Shmaya, we are transitioning from the Avot. From *Parashat Lech Lecha* until *Parashat Vayishlach*, we dealt with three leaders and fathers: Avraham, Yitzchak, and Yaakov. The beginning of our parashah reads, "אלה תולדות יעקב יוסף בן שבע עשרה שנה—This, then, is the line of Yaakov: Yosef who was seventeen years of age," meaning that these are the descendants of Yaakov.[1] It's important to note that when the

---

1   *Bereishit* 37:2.

Torah says, "*eileh toldot*," our expectation is that it is about to tell us the line of descendants, since this is the translation of the word *toldot*. But, with the main characters in *Sefer Bereishit*, the word *toldot* is not only about their children, but also about defining their identities. For example, after "*eileh toldot Noach*" we might expect the names of Noach's children to follow, but instead the *pasuk* continues, "נח איש צדיק תמים היה בדורתיו—Noach was a *tzaddik* in his generation."[2] Another example would be, "ואלה תולדות יצחק בן אברהם, אברהם הוליד את יצחק"—This is the story of Yitzchak, son of Avraham, Avraham begot Yitzchak."[3] However, when we get to "*eileh toldot Yaakov*," it's followed by the name of Yosef. We know that's not true though, because Yaakov had twelve sons. This means that the Torah must be presenting some insight about the relationship between Yaakov and Yosef.

Yosef is a very mysterious character because it seems as if he's not acting properly. He appears to be challenging and difficult. Yosef portrayed himself as a leader. This could seem at first glance like *ga'avah*, haughtiness, but at the same time Yosef never sins or fails. He openly says to all around him that his success is from Hashem and not himself. For these reasons, the character of Yosef is very mysterious to us.

The second level of this mystery regarding Yosef is where do we position him? He is not recognized as one of the Avot, yet the Torah emphasizes his story as if he is one of the Avot. The main character after Avraham is Yaakov, and the main character after Yaakov—is Yosef. The Torah puts very little focus on Yitzchak, to the extent that based on the structure of the Torah, the three Avot might be Avraham, Yaakov, and Yosef. The entire last fourteen *perakim* of *Sefer Bereishit* revolve around one character, and that character is Yosef.

In a way, Yosef got a level up because he was not really one of the *shevatim*, and he was close to Yaakov. More importantly than that, his life was very similar to Yaakov's stories.

1. Yaakov was hated by his brother, and Yosef too was hated by his brothers.

---

2   *Bereishit* 6:9.
3   *Bereishit* 25:19.

2. Yaakov was thrown out of the land, and Yosef too was thrown out of the land after being cast away into a pit full of scorpions and snakes.

The similarities can go on and when the Torah states, "אלה תולדות יעקב יוסף—This, then, is the line of Yaakov: Yosef."[4] It is telling us that, on a superficial level, there are a lot of similarities between Yaakov and Yosef. Now we must ask the question, what is the link between Yaakov and Yosef?

In order to help us understand who Yosef really was, the *Sefat Emet* explains[5] regarding "בית יעקב אש ובית יוסף להבה—And the house of Yaakov shall be a fire, and the house of Yosef a flame,"[6] that they were both part of the fire. But the *pasuk* makes a distinction that Yaakov is the fire and Yosef is the flames. So, you look at the *pasuk* and you ask: What is this all about? We see that even though on the superficial level Yaakov and Yosef seem to be the same, when we dive into their characters, they are total opposites. Whenever Yaakov goes through obstacles, there is change. He struggled with Eisav, and there was a change. He struggled with Lavan, and there was a change. He struggled with Shimon and Levi, and there was a change. The change that occurs is always linked to Yaakov. His name was changed, his wife was changed, and his way of looking at reality changed. So, Yaakov is transformed; he changes and he develops. He is the result of the heat and wind that surround him.

With Yosef, it's different. He is always affecting others. He is always talking about others. He is always relating to others. If you think about his name, it comes from the word *l'hosif*, to add. He is always affecting other people, affecting society, and changing the world. There has always been in Jewish history, just one Jewish person who in his essence was leading the entire world, and that was Yosef. His identity is that the obstacles don't change him, but instead demand of him to change others. He goes on to change Mitzrayim, his brothers, his father, and Binyamin, and it will change history; it will change agriculture; and it

---

4   *Bereishit* 37:2.
5   In the year 1873.
6   *Ovadiah* 1:18.

will change the economy. Yosef is the concept of *lehavot*, of flames, of moving outward, of effecting change.

I think there is something much more powerful here. The mystery of Yosef is: When should one use their ability to affect others? There is an amazing Midrash that states that Yosef didn't fail. It asks how did Yosef not fail with *eishet Potiphar*? The Midrash answers that he saw the face of his father. There is something much deeper about this Midrash. It is saying that the *lehavah* knows that he is a *lehavah*. A flame knows that he is a flame, and therefore, he is not the coal, and he is not the charcoal. He is not the secret of the fire, but an extension of the fire. His only ability is to know that he has someone greater to look up to.

When we look at our generation, we are so often talking about changing the world. The truth is that you don't know the world. Sometimes we confuse the *lehavah* with the *aish*. We are trying to affect our friends, affect society and affect the world, but we don't have any core. People are talking about changing the world, yet they don't even know themselves and who they are. People are talking about transforming the world, when they never had a conversation with their children. People are giving *shiurim* about the importance of education, but they never have the time to educate themselves. Yosef is the transition from the Avot to Moshe Rabbeinu because he was teaching that we have a responsibility to affect the world—on condition. You are only allowed to affect the world if you remember "דמות דיוקנו של אביו"—the image of the face of his father."[7] You must remember that you are the *lehavah* of something else; if you don't have the *aish* then your *lehavah* will die out. You cannot become an extension, if you don't have an extension cord connecting you back to the source. Yaakov was the source, and then Yosef said: my definition of struggle is not to change me, it's to affect others, because I know that I am always *toldot Yaakov*.

The berachah as we enter Shabbat and sit at the table with our family is to look around and realize that the secret of people that affect

---

7   *Sefat Emet, Bereishit, Vayeishev* 17.

outward is that they are the people that take the time to tune inward before going outward.

LIVING THE LEARNING

Who is your "gas station" in life that enables or excites you to continue the energy they have given you to affect those around you?

Parashat Vayeishev

CHANUKAH: IMPERFECT

ON CHANUKAH, we celebrate winning the war against the Greeks. The question we have to ask ourselves is: What were the Greeks about? There are different ideas, although one of them was that they wanted to show how man was perfect. If you look at pictures from Greek culture, you will see images of the "perfect man." They portray man as a god, and as perfect. They celebrate man as a being that can do anything and everything.

There was one mitzvah in the Jewish culture that particularly bothered the Greeks: the mitzvah of *brit milah*. The mitzvah of *brit milah* is really the antithesis of the Greeks. The mitzvah of *brit milah* says to man at his first moment in the world, "You were born, and you are not perfect." You need to change yourself, recognize that you are not accomplished, finished, or the end product. Man has a lot of things he needs to improve and perfect. When man is created it says "וייצר יְ-הוה אלקים את האדם—The Lord, God, formed man."[1] *Rashi* addresses why there are two *yudim* in the word *vayitzer*. He explains that it is because man, even before the sin, was created with a *yetzer hara* and a *yetzer hatov*, which together are represented by the two *yudim*. Although man was created with a *yetzer hara*—and he is therefore not perfect, nor is he God—still, man might even be 99 percent complete, yet he is not, nor can he ever be, 100 percent complete. No matter how great he is, he is not the greatest.

---

1   *Bereishit* 2:7.

61

That is the mitzvah of *brit milah*, and what the Greeks were fighting against. They wanted to diminish the idea of man being imperfect. If someone was born with an imperfection, they would throw them off a cliff into the ocean. The Jews do not say or do this. We say, "We are imperfect." We smile because we do not know. We smile because we have questions. We celebrate the fact that night is part of the world and questions are part of life.

When we celebrate Chanukah, something incredible happens. The Gemara in *Masechta Shabbat* 21b says that "מצות חנוכה נר איש וביתו—The mitzvah of Chanukah is for a person, and his household, to light a candle." The one holiday that you cannot celebrate without a home is Chanukah? But why? Why can it not be celebrated in the *shuk*, or outside in the streets? Why do we need to go home? What does this have to do with Chanukah? It would seemingly make sense to go to the Beit Hamikdash for *aliyah l'regel* or to celebrate in the streets and light up the night with candles? Why do we have to go home?

The home is the place in the world where you can be imperfect. In the outside world, we show that we have knowledge and degrees. At home, no one puts up a poster saying, "We have degrees," but rather, they put up posters saying "We have garbage, a dirty floor, sibling struggles, spousal issues, and even fighting in the house." The home is the place that demonstrates to the Greeks that we are not afraid of the fact that we are not perfect. In our homes we struggle, and that's where we light our Chanukah candles. We light our Chanukah candles in the home because it is a place where we recognize that we cannot do everything. The house is where we need to sleep, to rest, and show our lack of perfection. It is where we celebrate the fact that we are imperfect.

My berachah as we enter *Parashat Vayeishev* is that we go into Chanukah and are able to recognize that there are people in the world who only want to show the image, but are not able to be self-aware or honest. Chanukah is about being honest and aware. *B'ezrat Hashem*, when we are going home, we should walk into our *batim*, houses, and look at the fact that we are aware of who we are and are happy about the fact that we are not perfect.

CHANUKAH: OUTSIDE IN

LEARNING CONVERSATION

I want to start with a halachah from Chanukah and then relate it to the first *pasuk* of our parashah. This halachah teaches where we light the Chanukah candles. When we think about where we do something, we know that the place where we do something will have an effect on the action we're doing. For example, we get married in a beautiful location because we want it to affect the emotional setting of the wedding. The same is true when we choose where to light the Chanukah candles. The halachah conveys a message of how we should view the candles through the location in which we're lighting them.

In *Masechta Shabbat* it says, "מצות נר חנוכה פתח ביתו מבחוץ—It is a mitzvah to place the Chanukah lamp at the entrance to one's house on the outside, so that all can see it."[1] The place where we light the candles are "*petach beito mi'bachutz.*" The way we understand these three words helps us understand the purpose of the Chanukah candles. What is *petach beito*, the door of one's house? It is the border between your family and the world. It's the place of tension between the comfort of your family and discomfort, fear, tension, and difficulty of the greater world. But the Gemara adds in another word. Not only is it *petach beito*, at the door of one's house, but it needs to be *mi'bachutz*, outside—that the direction is to be aware of the tension yet direct the candles outward from the home. So why is it important for the candles to be outside? I think there's a very strong answer.

---

1   *Shabbat* 21b.

I think we often view the outside world as a problem. We go there if we need to, but it's something that we stay away from. But our general vision of the outside is something that we need to overcome, not learn from, or grow in. Chanukah teaches us that the outside is an opportunity, and the Chanukah candles need to be outside because there's something you need to internalize about the outside.

The outside exposes a person to questions. It exposes a person to vulnerability, to the feeling of: "I'm not sure where I am." Chanukah teaches you that outside is not a bad thing. What I learned from Yeshivat Otniel, where all the windows are made of glass, is that outside is something that we're aware of. The Piaseczna Rebbe says that every *beit midrash* needs to be aware of not just what's going on inside but the outside world as well. You can't remove yourself from the outside. Therefore, the Chanukah candles force us to understand that the outside is not a place that we run away from but a place that we have to embrace, that we can learn from and be a part of. Even if it's difficult, we need to know the outside.

In our parashah the *pasuk* says, "וישב יעקב בארץ מגורי אביו"—Now Yaakov settled in the land where his father had sojourned."[2] There are two things in this *pasuk* that are not needed. The word "*vayeishev*," settled, is not needed. Why? I need to know that he's in Israel. So, say Yaakov is in Eretz Canaan. The addition of the word *vayeishev* is teaching us that there's something going on here. The *Sefat Emet* says *vayeishev* is *bechinat Shabbat*, the aspect of Shabbat. The idea of *lashevet*, to sit, is a concept of Shabbat, of comfort, relaxation, and lack of struggle. Until now, he had *avodat kashot*, hard work. The *Sefat Emet*, based on *Rashi*, says the lifestyle of Yaakov was to struggle and fight against outside tensions, like Eisav, Lavan, and Shechem. But now he wants to transition to *vayeishev*, being settled. He wants to go from the world of dealing with outside to go back to the world of Shabbat.

So comes the second part of the *pasuk* and says, "*b'eretz megurei aviv*—The land where his father had sojourned." Why not just say

---

2   *Bereishit* 37:1.

Eretz Canaan? He wanted to go back to the world of his father Yitzchak, where he didn't need to struggle. The first *pasuk* of our parashah is about Yaakov wanting to go back home and being tired of struggling with the outside. And then immediately, we are told the story of Yosef. This means there is something that Hashem was trying to teach Yaakov. His uniqueness allowed him to go outside. He wanted to go to the aspect of *vayeishev*, calmness, but Hashem didn't want him to. Hashem wanted Yaakov to teach the Jewish people that there was something to learn, gain, and embrace from going into the world of Eisav, Lavan, Shechem, and the struggles of Yosef with his brothers.

I think that we see here this same idea of Chanukah *mi'bachutz*. The idea of Chanukah is to understand that so often we run away from the outside, and Yaakov in this parashah wants to run away from the outside. And the lesson of this parashah connects with the story of Chanukah, which is to realize that we need to stop being dismissive of the outside questions. If in the outside world people are dealing with the issue of intermarriage, it has to be an inside question. If the world is struggling with the question of "Why learn Gemara?" it's a question we all need to be aware of. If we are dealing with "What does it mean to have a relationship?" that's not an outside question, it's an inside question. If people are struggling with their responsibilities to family and dedication, that is no longer an outside question. The outside is teaching us to redefine our inside world.

So, my berachah as we enter into this Shabbat and Chanukah is to not run away from the struggles of what the world is presenting us with, but to embrace the questions, to learn the questions, and to bring them back into our homes so that we can redefine our homes into not just places that run away from the outside but are aware of the outside, and can therefore affect the outside.

CHANUKAH: YEARNING

*Rav Yair follows the Sefat Emet to explain the idea
behind hilchot Chanukah.*

"Trying is succeeding; succeeding is image."

OPENING QUESTIONS

1. If you would have to celebrate the miracle of Chanukah, how would you do it? What mitzvot or halachot would enable you to continue the memory of the Chanukah miracle?
2. Contract and compare the mitzvot and halachot of Chanukah to your list in question one.
3. Why do we light in the entrance to our homes?
4. Why in the mitzvah of Chanukah is there *mehadrin min ha'mehadrin* more than any other mitzvot?
5. What is the symbolism of lighting our candles at such a low height?

LEARNING CONVERSATION

We want to focus this week on some of the ideas of Chanukah, and one of the most interesting things when we try to understand Chanukah is *hilchot Chanukah*. The reason that it is interesting is because at the end of the day there was a fight, and then there was oil, and then there was a miracle that lasted for eight days. Suddenly, the halachah walks in and adds all these details that seem to be insignificant and irrelevant. I want to focus on three of the halachot.

The first halachah is where we light the menorah: *Mitzvat Chanukah al hapetach.*[1] I know that we have gotten used to lighting Chanukah candles in the window, but really, according to the Gemara, that is not the ideal. That was only because of different ideas relating to *pirsumei nisa*, publicizing the miracle, but at the end of the day, the best *pirsumei nisa* is if the entrance of your home is facing toward the road. The best place to light Chanukah candles is *davka* at the entrance of one's home. The obvious question is, Who cares if you light the Chanukah candles in the middle of the road? If the message of the lighting is that "I am so interested in lighting up the world," then I should go onto a tank with a huge menorah and drive in the streets and light it there. What is this idea that halachah looks at Chanukah and says, "You know what the best thing to do is? Light your Chanukah candles at the entrance of your home."

Halachah number two and question number two is on the issue of *mehadrin*, and *mehadrin min ha'mehadrin.*[2] The Gemara says there are three levels of the mitzvah.[3] The most basic of the levels, which almost nobody does, is to light one candle only. Every night of Chanukah, just one candle is lit. The *mehadrin* or higher level is to light a candle according to the number of people in your household. The *mehadrin min ha'mehadrin*, or highest level, is that each person in the house lights their own menorah corresponding to the number of that night. We look at this concept, yet we find it nowhere else. True, by Sukkot we have this idea that with lulav, we have this idea of the mitzvah and the *mehadrin*. But there is only one mitzvah during the year that we have not just the mitzvah, not just *mehadrin*, but *mehadrin min ha'mehadrin*. So, the *Sefat Emet* questions, What is going on over here? What happened during Chanukah that suddenly you have this concept of better and better and better?

The third question is concerning the place where we light the Chanukah candles. The area where we light the Chanukah candles,

---

1   *Sefat Emet, Bereishit, Chanukah* 17.
2   Ibid.
3   *Shabbat* 21b.

ideally, should be below ten *tefachim*. The obvious question we are all asking is: Who cares? If you lit it above that, what does it matter?

We will first try to answer the question of why we should light below ten *tefachim*. The Gemara says that there is only one area of the world that Hashem never went into. On a basic level, it says the Hashem never went beneath ten *tefachim*.[4] So where do we light our Chanukah candles? Says the Gemara in Shabbat that ideally you should light your Chanukah candles below ten *tefachim*. There is no other mitzvah that we do below ten *tefachim*.

Let's put all three of our questions and halachot together. The first was that we light in the entrance; the second was that we have this concept of mitzvah, *mehadrin*, and *mehadrin min ha'mehadrin*; and third was that we light underneath ten *tefachim*. The *Sefat Emet* takes all three of these halachot and connects them to one main message of what Chanukah is all about. He says you have to realize that this idea is, "כי בודאי בימים הללו נפתח שערי בינה וקדושה רק כפי עבודת האדם‎—It is certain that during these praiseworthy days the gates of understanding are opened, and holiness is only in accordance with the effort man puts in."[5] He says that Chanukah is a celebration of what people decided to try and put effort into. It is about the fact that they tried. The concept that Chanukah is teaching us is that it's not about what was given to us, but it's about where we took an active role to make things better. Based on this mindset of Chanukah, we can understand the three halachot we brought.

The idea of the *petach*, entrance, is incredible because the first time we find the word *petach* in Tanach is with Avraham Avinu. What is interesting about the *petach* is that it defines a mindset. The mindset linked with the home is relaxation. When it is Shabbat, you go home because it's about *menuchah*. So, what is the "concept" of the *petach*? Says the *Sefat Emet*, the *petach* is a place of yearning. Why was Avraham sitting "*petach ohel*—at the entrance of his tent"?[6] Avraham was sitting

---

4   *Sukkah* 4b.
5   *Sefat Emet, Bereishit*, Chanukah 17.
6   *Bereishit* 18:1.

at the entrance because he was yearning. We have to understand that if you are yearning, it changes you. A person who is yearning is different from a person who isn't yearning. This is something that will not be seen in the action, but in the reaction. This means that a lot of people might daven. Some people might come a minute late, and others will come a minute early. A person that comes a minute late and whose mindset is to walk in as late as possible will not be yearning. They will open the same siddur, and they will say the same words. But their reaction to the *tefillah* will be, "When is this going to be over?" This proves that the yearning defines the action. Now, if someone came in a minute early and just sat there for a minute and got excited about the davening, the action will result in a strong effect on the person. The idea of lighting the candles in the *petach* is expressing the demand of Chanukah. It is asking us, are you a person who is yearning? Are you sitting on the *petach*? Or are you a person that is hiding inside? Are you looking for comfort and for what's easy? Or are you ready for the *petach*? The *Sefat Emet* tells us that this is exactly why we light in the entrance of our homes. The candles are not asking us what are you doing, but what are you *yearning* to do?

The second halachah is about idea of mitzvah, *mehadrin*, and *mehadrin min ha'mehadrin*. The actual mitzvah is so simple. The reason it is so simple is because all you need is one candle. However, someone who is yearning for greatness will say, "You know what? It's not enough. I don't want just one candle, I want one for every person in my house. You know what? I want to feel the difference in every single day so that the first day of Chanukah is not like the third night." When someone is a yearning person it's not just about the objective, it's about how I want that experience. As a result, we make a new berachah every night even though it's the same action. Then the mitzvah will become *mehadrin min ha'mehadrin* because you were yearning.

So, what is the third and final halachah? We must ask: How do we know if a person is yearning? It is only if they are willing to go into the most challenging place which is below ten *tefachim*. Symbolically, underneath ten *tefachim* represents where you feel the least connection with Hashem. That's where we light the candles, because we must be able to turn those areas into a feeling of yearning. Yes, Hashem, I don't understand. I don't understand why there is difficulty in the world; I don't understand why there's a soldier in Israel that gets stabbed; I don't understand any of it! But the idea of Chanukah is to go in there and yearn. Yearn for the world to be different! Yearn to make an effect! Yearn to make a difference!

I think these three halachot, that really have nothing to do with the oil, reveal to us what Chanukah does. Chanukah teaches us through the halachot of Chanukah that sometimes the opportunity of the winter—the season when Chanukah falls out—is that people need to understand that cold and snow and rain demands of us to ask what type of person we are. Are we someone who is yearning? Or are you someone who just does actions?

The berachah as we enter into *Parashat Mikeitz* is to learn from Yosef the dreamer. Yosef is the character of Chanukah because when he got thrown into a pit, he yearned. When he was thrown into another pit, he yearned again. When his brothers finally reached him, Yosef didn't give them a solution, he wanted them to yearn too. If you are yearning, then your actions change and don't just remain an action, but they become a relationship that can change the actor.

LIVING THE LEARNING

Call a teacher from your younger years and ask them what they thought you'd be when you got older. What were you yearning for when you were in the great stage of a yearning child?

MISSING OIL IS THE BEGINNING

LEARNING CONVERSATION

We just lit candles here in the Old City with hundreds of people giving out candies. Just above us there was a sign that said "*Neis gadol hayah poh*—a great miracle happened here." With that in mind, I want to share a short idea on Chanukah. The Gemara in *Masechta Shabbat* deals with Chanukah. There's a *sugya* in the middle of this discussion that seems to be unrelated to Chanukah. It mentions a verse in our parashah: "והבור ריק אין בו מים—The pit was empty, but that there was no water," describing the scene when the brothers throw Yosef into the pit. The Gemara teaches us that the pit was empty, but that there was no water. Why do we say that it's empty *and* missing water? It's redundant! The Chassidic Master Rav Doni Sausen explains as follows: What's interesting about the story of Yosef is that in the beginning, he had everything. He was living in his father's home and had his father's love. He had the dreamcoat and a great destiny. But at the same time, he was also missing friendships and relationships. Then his brothers threw him into the pit, this empty pit. The verse could literally be describing the pit, but it could also be describing the experience Yosef was going through.

Suddenly he's in a place that's empty. There are no more brothers, and there is no more father—no more destiny, and no more dreams—*ein bo mayim*. He was experiencing "*ein*." Everything was empty; everything was gone. But what Rav Sausen was teaching is that *mayim*, water, is life. Yosef didn't even have that. He was so lost and so gone. What's interesting is that the moment when he lost everything is the moment he gained everything. In the beginning, the Jewish people also had so much, and the Greeks took it all away from them. Maybe this is why it's linked to Chanukah. They took away our oil, sanctuary, Torah, land, family and mitzvot. Everything that we had was gone.

So often when we see that something is missing, we think it is the end of the story. But that's not true. What we learn from the pit is that when things are *"ein"* is when you begin to build a new story. I think that the story of Chanukah shows us that there are many times when we feel the darkness. We feel the lack and the absence, and we feel the story has ended. Chanukah's real miracle is when we realize that when we think the story is over is when it really begins.

I started by mentioning that we just lit Chanukah candles outside. *Neis gadol hayah poh.* This year and the last three months, I lost many things. I lost the opportunity to be in yeshiva a lot. I lost the opportunity to sing and dance a lot. I lost the opportunity to go to shul and learn a lot. A lot of things I had were suddenly gone. But at the same time, while I lit the candles, I realized that it's also the beginning of a new story, of the next story.

My berachah as we enter into *Parashat Mikeitz* is that whenever or wherever we feel the emptiness of the pit or the lack of Chanukah oil, we should know that though it might seem externally like it's the end of a story, internally it's part of a new story.

Parashat Vayigash

CHANUKAH: GROW

Rosh Chodesh Tevet, Chanukah

> "Down is the inner up, and up can be the inner down."

OPENING QUESTIONS

1. What prophecy do you think Hashem should have given to Am Yisrael to prepare them for 210 years of exile?
2. What enables a person to grow in places that are broken?
3. What is the right mindset to have in challenging places?

LEARNING CONVERSATION

One of the *pesukim* in our parashah is overlooked. The *pasuk* is a regular *nevuah*, prophecy, that God gave to Yaakov. We can only understand the depth of it by understanding the historical context it was given in.

Yosef told Yaakov that he wanted him to come down to Egypt. Yaakov's grandfather, Avraham Avinu, had a dream that when the Jews go down to Egypt that is when exile would begin.[1] Yaakov clearly knew from the moment he made the decision to go down to Mitzrayim, that although things might look good for a short amount of time, slowly but surely, they would eventually enter into slavery. On Yaakov's way down to Egypt, knowing that this was the beginning of a great darkness, he received a *nevuah*. In the *nevuah*, Hashem said to Yaakov, "אנכי ארד עמך

---

1   *Bereishit* 15.

73

מצרימה ואנכי אעלך גם עלה—I will go down with you, and I will take you up and up."[2]

This leaves us with a few questions. The first is obviously if you are going to go up, then you are going to go down, so why do you have to emphasize that you are going to go down? Yaakov knows that he is going into exile. Just tell me, Hashem, that You will come back with me, and You'll hold my hand, and everything will be fine. This is like taking your kid on the first day of first grade and telling him, "I will pick you up after school, everything is going to be okay." Why did Hashem need to say "*Anochi ered imcha*—I am going to go down with you"?

The second question is why did Hashem say "*Anochi a'alecha gam aloh*—I will take you up and up"? Just say it once! What's the need for the repetition of going up and up?

It's important to answer these questions in order to understand something very simple. From that *pasuk* and for the next 210 years, there would not be one word uttered from God to man. In all the years of physical abuse, slavery, and murder that the Jews suffered, they did not hear one more time God's name. They did not hear His voice; they did not have a Torah; and they did not have a land. All they had was this one sentence. This sentence is obviously more than what we think of it. This was going to play as the message of how to deal with 210 years of not knowing where God was. The *Sefat Emet* comments on "*havtachah l'dorot*" that this means that the *pasuk* was not speaking to Yaakov only; it was addressed to all the Jews—anyone who had to leave for Egypt, anyone who has to leave comfort, anyone who has to leave *abba* and *imma*, anyone who has to leave anything simple, anyone who has to enter into darkness, anyone who has to light Chanukah candles in the darkest nights of the year.[3] Hashem said, "I am going to go down with you." He did not mention Yaakov's name, because "*Anochi ered imcha*" means "I will go down with all of you into those difficult situations." The *Sefat Emet* continues, "כי כל מצור לאיש ישראל רק לטובה להיות אח״כ יתרון." Every experience of going downward is only for some

---

2   *Bereishit* 46:4.
3   *Sefat Emet, Bereishit, Vayigash* 2. From the year 1872.

greater good that only later will be gained. This is all on condition that you are willing to go down to Mitzrayim and how you enter Mitzrayim, and this depends on your mindset. The *Sefat Emet* tells us that a lot of people think that you have to overcome the challenge. Just get into that struggle and then get out of it, so everything will be good. According to the *Sefat Emet*, Hashem was telling Yaakov: No! I want you to know that down there is where I really am. Stop trying to overcome; stop trying to erase the problem; stop trying to run away from Egypt. I want you to realize that Egypt is where the Jews will be born. This will happen when they realize that it's not to overcome, but it's to become even greater. Hashem says I am going down because you will grow more throughout this experience, and that was God's message to the Jewish people for 210 years. Stop reminiscing; stop living somewhere else; stop thinking that someone and somewhere will be the solution. I want you to be the solution. This is why Hashem emphasizes that He is going down with them to Mitzrayim—that once you are in Mitzrayim, see it as a conversation between you and Hashem. This is the reason that Hashem said He would go back up and up. The goal wasn't to return to the light up, but rather to experience the down in its fall, and then the up wouldn't just be up, it would be much greater. Since your character changes when you are down, the up will be more than an external happiness but will become a revelation of inner joy.

My berachah is to realize that Asarah B'Tevet, the tenth of Tevet, comes out immediately after Chanukah. This chronological order could be revealing a great message to us. Maybe Asarah B'Tevet was the result of our wrong mindset of Chanukah.

Asarah B'Tevet is when all of our enemies decided that they would destroy us because we perceived Chanukah in the wrong way. Chanukah's message is to not be afraid. Chanukah's message is to realize that in those places like Egypt, you must not try and make it into something that it is not. I remember when I was in the army for nine months. I tried to make the army into yeshiva. I was miserable and cried every single night. Suddenly, I realized that the uniqueness of the army is social. I then decided to give out chocolates every morning and, with that decision, my entire army experience changed. When I embraced the place that I was in, I was able to grow—not to just get out of there, but to *aloh a'aleh*, go up and up. The question was: Why does Hashem say I'll go down? Because I want you to stop looking up, just go down and be where you are. If you are in Mitzrayim, be in Mitzrayim. If you are in Tzfat, be in Tzfat. If you are in a class in high school, be in high school. If you are in Israel, be in Israel. Only then, will you not just overcome, but you will grow *aloh a'aleh*, up and up.

LIVING THE LEARNING

Build a Lego structure with some young children, then break it, and when they are crying ask them what can they build new with these new pieces.

BIG MOMENTS

THERE ARE MOMENTS in Jewish history that are so primary and so exalted that we really have to figure out how to translate it into our lives. There are two big moments in history that we see in this parashah. One of them is the moment that Yehudah meets Yosef. It's a moment where things could go all the way down and the entire Jewish story could end, or things could go all the way up and everything could be saved. The other moment is where Yaakov, a father who was yearning to see his child for twenty-two years, sees Yosef again. I think from both of these moments, we can learn a tremendous secret about Am Yisrael's story.

When Yehudah approached Yosef, it was such an exalted moment but the conversation was very complicated. Yehudah said, "Yosef, you said to us X and we said to you Y." He basically just repeated the story of what Yosef had said and what the brothers answered him. We take a step back and say, "Yehudah, are you serious? You are going into the deepest moment, and you can lose your brother right now! How in the world is that the way you approach this situation? Give him something new! Give him some new information! Tell him I am going to kill you if you don't give me back my brother! Tell him I am going to have a world war against Egypt if you don't give me back my brother! Be a little more aggressive! Really? You just tell him 'hey you said X and we said this?'" That is a big question we have on this moment of interaction between Yehudah and Yosef.

I think that if we really think about it, Yehudah is teaching us a very deep secret. We always think that in order to make changes we need something new, but really when we add new things, we become limited because it means that we lost the old. We lost what was, and we're looking for the next, and the next, and the next, which means that we've given up on before, and before, and before. We can see it in the world that we live in today, that we're so ready for new things, and we're so bored from the old. It means that we have to let go. Yehudah said to Yosef, "I am not adding any new information. All I'm saying to you is let's revive the past. Let's rethink what was. Let's go through the past instead of adding new things." Suddenly the whole story changed. They were not adding any new information, he was just giving him the story of what was, and that is the moment that Yosef revealed himself to the brothers. He also reveals to us that the secret of change is to stop doing new things and start looking differently at the things that are. Stop looking for the new Mashiach that's going to come and start looking at our children as Mashiach. Stop looking into what the next big moment will be and start looking at what's right in front of us with a new perspective.

The same applies with the second big moment of our parashah. We know that it says that Yaakov sees the *agalot* and suddenly he is revived. So, *Rashi* asks, What was it about these *agalot* that they were able to revive Yaakov? *Rashi* answers that Yaakov remembers that the last thing he learned with Yosef was *eglah arufah*. What revived him was the memory of the new perspective on the learning. He learned *eglah arufah* twenty-two years ago and now he's looking at it not as an ending, but as the beginning. That same *eglah* that was the last thing he learned with Yosef is now showing him that what he perceived as the end, he needs to perceive as the beginning. Yaakov changed his mindset. The *eglah* wasn't the end of the story, it was the beginning of the next stage. Yaakov was revived. He could only go and meet his son once he realized that he needed to look at things differently.

The berachah of this parashah is encapsulated in the two great and exalted moments of Yehudah convincing Yosef, and of Yaakov reuniting with his son. If we cannot look differently at what is, then nothing new will ever bring happiness to our lives.

Parashat Vayechi

AFFECT REDEMPTION

THIS SHABBAT we reach the end of *Sefer Bereishit*, but it's also a beginning. When we look at the parashah, we see something we only find here. Every single parashah in the Torah before it begins has white space. There is no break separating *Parashat Vayigash* from *Parashat Vayechi*.

Rashi explains that this is the beginning of exile. He says that because of exile, the hearts and eyes of Am Yisrael were already closed, as they were expecting the beginning of slavery. As such, this white space, known as a closed parashah, *parashat stumah*, represents the closing of the hearts and eyes of Am Yisrael. But I think that if you look deeper, the *Sefat Emet* teaches us an amazing idea.

He asks an incredible question: How should we define exile? So often we define exile as a place, but the *Sefat Emet* presents us with a much deeper understanding of what exile is really about. The *Sefat Emet* says, "העניין להראות שבני ישראל עושים רושם."[1] What is the whole concept? The eyes of Am Yisrael were shut, and therefore the Torah was shut. The core idea behind the lack of a space was to teach Am Yisrael about their ability to affect. Maybe that is the antithesis of what exile is all about. According to the definition of the *Sefat Emet*, exile is when you lose the feeling of affecting, when you feel like your sorrow doesn't affect anyone else.

I spent a lot of months in the hospital, and I felt alone. I was by myself, crying at night, trying to figure out how to get through the night.

---

1   *Sefat Emet, Bereishit, Vayechi* 14:4.

I didn't see or feel like it affected me, but then I heard my parents, wife, and children. I realized that my pain has an impact on other people.

Not that it's a good thing, but it means that you will be impacting others all the time. When you lose that emotion, when you lose that feeling, when you lose that mindset, that is exile.

As we enter into *Parashat Vayechi*, one of the last messages that I think *Sefer Bereishit* is leaving with us is the message of the book itself. Individuals can have an effect on others before a nation does. *Sefer Shemot* will begin the journey of our nation, but *Sefer Bereishit* was filled with journeys of individuals. The Torah did that on purpose. We don't want to have a nation that teaches individuals that they can't affect others.

My berachah as we enter into the last parashah of *Sefer Bereishit* is that whatever you're going through, whether it's happiness or if you're standing under a chuppah, you are affecting the Beit Hamikdash. And if, *chas v'shalom*, you're going through challenges or difficulties, you are affecting the entire circle of Am Yisrael. It might be difficult, but when you feel that you're making a difference, it will be the beginning of the journey to *geulah*.

Parashat Vayechi

SPACE

WE KNOW THAT the *Ramban* calls *Sefer Shemot*, "*Sefer galut v'geulah*—The book of exile and redemption."[1] But a lot of times, we have to ask ourselves: What is exile? On the basic level, exile is a place. On a deeper level exile is concept, a mindset, and a lifestyle. Exile is that you might be somewhere, even in front of the Kotel, but you are still in exile. You might be in the presence of greatness, but still in exile. When we enter *Parashat Vayechi*, there is something that happens that is different than in any other parashah in the entire Torah. In every parashah, when it ends, there is a space before the next parashah begins. However, when we get to *Parashat Vayechi*, it begins right from *Parashat Vayigash*. *Rashi* says this is the moment that *galut* started. So, the question we have to ask ourselves is: Could it be that *Rashi* is saying—based on the Midrash—that the lack of a space is the definition of the beginning of exile? If you want to say that exile is when everyone leaves the land, then that is easy to understand. And if you want to say that exile means that you are a slave to Pharaoh, then this too is easy to understand. But does it make sense to say that exile starts when Yaakov is alive, Yosef is alive, and the dream is alive?

The *pasuk* in *Vayigash* then says great things: "ויפרו וירבו מאד—and they were fertile and increased greatly."[2] The Jewish people were prospering; everything looked great. *Rashi* says that although externally there was so much success, internally the exile started when there is no space. So, the question that the *Sefat Emet* asked in 1871 is: What is the symbolism

---

1   *Ramban* on *Shemot*, Introduction 1.
2   *Bereishit* 47:27.

of this space? He then says something incredible: The letters are what are given to us by Hashem, and the space is what leaves room for man to get involved. He says that in every parashah, Hashem takes a step back and leaves room for us to get involved, to ask questions, and to be creative. However, there is one parashah where there is no such space. There is no involvement. There is no input. That is exile, says *Rashi*. The *Sefat Emet* says that exile begins the moment you become. One might be surrounded by lights, but if you are not involved, active, and giving input, then even though you may be surrounded by greatness, you are living in exile.

There was one time that I asked myself: What is the greatest struggle of the modern day? A lot of people call it laziness, but this is not true. People are constantly doing. But whenever they are confronted with a reality that is slightly complicated, they become passive. Our problem is not laziness; it is that if people say something is complicated, the game is over. If things are difficult, they go to sleep. If people are questioned, they become silent. This is exile. Exile is where you stop being involved.

My berachah as we enter *Parashat Vayechi* is that we should understand, realize, and recognize that exile is not just a place, but is the way you view yourself. Are you controlled by reality? Do you feel you can't make a difference? If yes, then you are in exile. Then Pharoah will come, and the world will fall apart. Whenever you realize that you are the space, that you can be involved, add, interpret, and question, then you will be in the world of redemption. So, the berachah this Shabbat is that we should create space and realize that places that are a void are not problems, but rather they are opportunities for us to get involved and to spread the concept that we do not just watch things, we get involved in them.

Parashat Shemot

THE OPPORTUNITY OF CHALLENGE

THIS SHABBAT we enter into *Parashat Shemot*, into *Sefer Shemot*, and there are a lot of things that are going on. One thing we have to try to understand is the name of the book. The name of the book in English is "Exodus." Exodus is translated in Hebrew as *shichrur*, which means "the experience of leaving Egypt." It is a beautiful name, but what is difficult about it is that it is only telling the story from *perek aleph* to *perek yud gimmel*. From *yud-gimmel*, or one could even argue from *k'riat Yam Suf*, *Sefer Shemot* is not dealing with leaving Egypt. Therefore, the Hebrew name chosen for the book is not Exodus; it is *Shemot*. Thus comes the *Sefat Emet* in 1871 and wants to understand why this is the name of the book. He brings a *pasuk* from *Kohelet* 7:1, "טוב שם משמן טוב—A good name is greater than good oil." The *Sefat Emet* then tries to explain what the symbolism is between a name and oil. He says that oil is a position that is given to a person. Where do we learn this from? In the Torah, how are Kohanim and *melachim*, kings, anointed? The way they are appointed is by having oil poured on them. By pouring oil on them, we are really saying something amazing to them. We are saying that oil is something that does not go in; it is different than water. We are telling the *melech* not to get too full of himself. *Shemen*, oil, is something that is on you; it is beyond you. You do not deserve more because you are a king. You do not get more because you are a king. You do not get to ask people to do you favors because you are a king. You have to recognize that your position is on you and is something that demands responsibility from you. It is not something that you earned, or that you deserved. This is the *shemen*.

But what is the *sheim*, the name? The *sheim* is not what is given to you as a position, but it is what is created by you. This is in you. He explains that a name is not only something that your parents gave you, it is something that you create for yourself. He says that there is an amazing thing to look at in Tanach. In Tanach we know that there are different people who went into fire. We know that Nadav and Avihu went into the fire, and they never come out. The *Sefat Emet* says they are *shemen tov*, good oil. They had the *kehunah*, but it was on them. Then, when they were confronted with fire, the game was over. It was done, since something that is on you does not define you. Just because you wear tzitzit doesn't mean you are religious. Just because you put on tefillin, it does not make you religious. Just because you light Shabbos candles, it does not make you a Jewish person. They are on you, but this does not make them in you. Therefore, when Nadav and Avihu had the *kehunah* that was brought to them via the oil and they were confronted by the fire, it consumed them. We also have Mishael, Azarya, and Chananya. They were never given a position. They were never Kohanim or *melachim*. Yet, they built, and built, and built even more. They were also thrown into a bonfire, but they came out alive! The *Sefat Emet* says that there is something about the name that is greater than the *shemen*. We are always looking for *shemen*; we are looking for degrees, titles. But what makes you incredible is what you built, not what you were given. *Shemen*, oil, is given, but a *sheim*, a name, is built, and Mitzrayim is the fire.

What we want to realize in *Sefer Shemot* is that the reason we went to Mitzrayim was to create names. This is because if you have a name, then when you are in Egypt you will become a nation. The introduction to *Shemot* is that we went to Mitzrayim with only seventy people. Yet we left with three million. How did this happen? How did we not disappear? This happened because we had names. The Midrash says that no matter what happened in exile, we never forgot our names. If someone is capable of building and being involved, then even Mitzrayim is an opportunity.

My blessing as we go into *Sefer Shemot* and into the journey of *Shovavim*, is that we should recognize that we have to stop looking for the *shemen* that is on us, and instead, we have to look for the *sheim* that is in us and defines us.

Parashat Shemot

IN MEMORY OF FOUR ANGELS

This is in memory of the 18th yahrzeit of Rav Yair's friends
from Otniel who were killed in a terrorist attack.
Their names were Gavriel, Tzvika, Yehuda, and Noam.

WHEN WE ENTER into *Sefer Shemot*, we are introduced to a very serious question: What enabled us to get through 210 years of slavery? We entered into the darkest period and the most difficult situation, but we got through it. The big question is, what allowed us to get through this experience?

I want to offer three possible answers to this question. The first is the first letter of the book, the second is the first word of the book, and the third is the main character of the book.

We would think that *Sefer Shemot* stands alone, but the first letter of *Sefer Shemot* is "*vav*." "ואלה שמות בני ישראל הבאים מצרימה את יעקב איש וביתו באו—And these are the names of the sons of Yisrael who came to Egypt with Yaakov, each coming with his household."[1] What would be the reason to start a new book with the letter of continuation? What are you continuing from? Similarly, in davening, we say about Yerushalayim, *v'l'Yerushalayim*—but what are we connecting this to? There are many different answers, but maybe the idea is to realize that there is never ever an option in life for something to stand alone. The reason that we fail is because we think that everything is in its own box. We don't view things as a chain reaction. We think that if we do something here it will have no impact there, and if we do something there it will have

---

1   *Shemot* 1:1.

no impact here. If we do something now it doesn't have anything to do with tomorrow, and if we do something tomorrow it's not because of yesterday. The first letter of *Shemot* teaches that nothing stands alone. The slavery is not an experience in of itself; it started a long time before. There were things that caused it, and there was even a *nevuah*, but the main theme is that we are not allowed to look at the misery that you're currently experiencing as something that is standalone. Instead, it is a chain reaction. Other people have been through this before you, and you are enabling yourself in this experience to enable others. Yes, it's not good to go through slavery but there will be others that will have to go through it, and you are going through it so that you can enable others. It is a chain-reaction of something great that was before, that's giving you the stamina to get through. Lesson number one is you cannot think that you're living in a box, rather you are living in a chain.

The second is the word *Shemot*. The word "*shem*" says the Midrash, "טוב שם משמן טוב—A good name is better than good oil."[2] The words *sheim*, name, and *shemen*, oil have the same first two letters. The difference is, *shemen* has the addition of the *nun*, and *shemen* is only used once you're appointed to a position. We appoint a king, and we anoint him with oil. When we appoint a Kohen, we also anoint him with oil. When we have a *Korban Minchah* we pour oil on it. *Shemen* is found in places that we are giving something over, like kingship, *korbanot*, and the *kehunah*. But as we learned from the *pasuk* in *Kohelet*, the name is greater than the position. So what? You have a title? It was given to you! A name is the way that you interact and think about yourself in relation to others. The *sheim* is what can get us through *galut*. We see Nadav and Avihu had *shemen* since they were appointed, but when they went into the fire of Hashem the game was over. We see Chananyah, Mishael, and Azaryia went into the fire also and they didn't have *shemen*, meaning they didn't have a title. What they had was a name, they had a *sheim*, so when they went into the fire, they were able to come out. The concept of *sheim* doesn't appear to be as great as *shemen*, but it could get us through the

---

2   *Kohelet* 7:1.

hard times. If all you're excited about is the *sheim*, the title, then when the fire comes the *shemen* ends. The *sheim* might be lower—it might be as exalted or great—but the name is something you built. The *sheim* is your awareness that you could affect others. If you believe that you could affect someone because of who you are, and not because of what you were given, then you can overcome any fire.

The third is Moshe Rabbeinu. We love talking about him, but he didn't talk. Moshe Rabbeinu was not somebody who conversed. Aharon needed to talk for him which means that Moshe was very much aware that his only real impact would have to come from self-improvement and not from his words because that was difficult for him. We think the more we talk, the more we express; the more we change, the better the world's going to become. But this is not true. Moshe Rabbeinu lived for eighty years in solitary confinement. No one knew of him, no one cared about him, and no one thought about him. Yet he became the greatest redeemer. If you don't know that the way you live is the only real impact you are making, then your impact will not be able to influence others and get them out of their state of misery. Moshe Rabbeinu is the character that says, "I am aware that the way I live is the only way to get people to believe." Every time he talked, no one listened. They didn't want to hear his words not because they were trivializing the situation but because words are dangerous. Words are something that we can just say, but you don't really have to do anything, and long-term they don't last. The third message is Moshe Rabbeinu was someone who wasn't talking all day, but rather was demanding of himself that if he wanted others to believe, then he had to believe in himself.

These are the first three insights into how we overcome Egypt and slavery: Number one is to never see things on their own and this is what the *vav* represents. Number two is to recognize that if we're making an impact through our names or through what we build, then we are not going to go anywhere. The third is that the real name that you have is not the words you say, or the books you write, but it's the recognition that what you want to demand of others, you have to be able to demand twice as much from yourself.

Parashat Va'eira

STOP IN THE NAME OF SHA-DDAI

> "A vulnerable leader is a true tour guide in life's maze."

OPENING QUESTIONS

1. In *Parashat Shemot*, Moshe says to Hashem: Why did you send me? What do you think is the deepest reason for Moshe's despair?
2. What are the differences between the leadership of the Avot and of Moshe? How did they reveal different perspectives on how Hashem interacts with the world?

LEARNING CONVERSATION

One of the most intense conversations in all of Tanach starts up at the end of last parashah and continues into this parashah. Hashem made the decision to send Moshe Rabbeinu to redeem the Jewish people. Moshe, with a naive mindset, said to himself that if Hashem said it, then it would happen. He walked into the fields, talked to the people, and not only did he not redeem them, but things got worse. He just said very simply to Hashem, "למה זה שלחתני—Why did You send me?"[1] Everything that you told me was a joke. Forget it all. I'm not interested in You, I'm not interested in the *shlichut*, and I don't want it at all. Hashem's response in the beginning of our parashah needs to be understood. The response was, "וארא אל אברהם אל יצחק ואל יעקב בא-ל-ל

---

1   *Shemot* 5:22.

88

ש-די ושמי ה' לא נודעתי להם—I appeared to Avraham, Yitzchak, and Yaakov as E-l Sha-ddai, but I did not make Myself known to them by My name Hashem."[2] To understand this, we need to ask two questions.

1. What is the difference between these two names? They knew the name of Sha-ddai, but they didn't know the name of Y-K-V-K? In order to understand this, we need to understand the difference between these two names.

2. How does this response have anything to do with what Moshe was talking about? How is this a response to Moshe's challenge to Hashem: why did You send me on this mission?

Rashi explains in *Sefer Bereishit* that the name of Sha-ddai expresses the idea of *dai*—enough. It comes from the idea that things need limits; things need to stop; and things can't be perfect. Anytime something in the world is not perfect, that is God's decision. If you are not a genius or if you are not a millionaire, it is not a mistake. When things seem imperfect because of their limitedness, this is known as the name of Sha-ddai. "שאמר לעולמו די—[Hashem] said to His world, 'Enough.'" This means that there will be moments, places, and times that you must experience *dai*—enough. This is when you are not getting exactly what you had thought. Y-K-V-K is Hashem's essence. This is when everything that you thought is exactly what happens. You thought you would marry Rachel, and you married Rachel. You thought you would marry Leah, and you married Leah. Whatever you expected is what happened. Those are two different experiences of the world, that are both the work of Hashem. The experience of Sha-ddai is where you experience the concept of *dai*, where what you wanted and what you got are different. This is not a mistake, but a Godly decision. There are other times where the experience will be that of Y-K-V-K, where what you wanted is exactly what you got, and that is what Hashem wanted you to experience.

Says the *Sefat Emet*, what does it mean that the name for the Avot was Sha-ddai and not of Y-K-V-K? The *Sefat Emet* explained that the

---

2   *Shemot* 6:2.

Avot were on the highest level.[3] Just practically speaking, they were the ones that started the journey. They spoke to Hashem constantly, and they were even on a higher level than Moshe Rabbeinu. The *Sefat Emet* tells us that if they had wanted to, they could have chosen to interact with the name of Hashem of Y-K-V-K. They didn't really have struggles because they weren't in Egypt; they weren't being inflicted, and they weren't being abused or murdered. They could've chosen to relate to Hashem as Y-K-V-K, with the view that everything is perfect, but the Avot didn't do this; they chose the other name of E-l Sha-ddai. This changed the whole story.

What was Hashem really saying to Moshe? He was saying that He needed him to realize that the Avot knew the difference, but still chose to use the name Sha-ddai. You, Moshe, have now experienced Sha-ddai, because what you expected didn't happen. You wanted the *shlichut* to work, and it didn't happen. So, your interpretation is I want Y-K-V-K because I want things to be perfect. I want things to be how they should be—that the generation will do what they should be doing. I don't want to see mistakes, and I don't want to see teenagers that are messing up. I am not interested in that. I want people to be in the right place. I want them to be Y-K-V-K. I want them to be sitting in the *beit midrash*; I want them to be with their families. I want them to be learning, and I want them to know priorities because that's the world that I want. Hashems heard all of this and said, "Now you have experienced the name of Sha-ddai. I want you to know that the Avot didn't see Sha-ddai as a problem; they chose it. They knew that wherever you find Y-K-V-K, it's true that you'll find Hashem, but you will not find people. It is in the places of Sha-ddai that you will find character. That's where you will find people, and that is where you will find greatness."

Yes, you can have an experience where everything is perfect, and you can look up and be amazed, inspired, and in awe, but you will not be a redeemer—you will be redeemed. You are reaching high up, but stepping on the flowers right under your feet.

---

3   In the year 1877.

Hashem was teaching Moshe Rabbeinu the deepest lesson of redemption: I don't want to redeem the Jews; I want them to redeem themselves. I want them to see Sha-ddai not as a problem or a mistake, but an opportunity.

My berachah as we enter into the *Parashat Va'eira* that we realize and understand that wherever we meet Sha-ddai, we should be excited for the opportunity to become the best character we can be.

LIVING THE LEARNING

Give three different people playdough and ask them to make a shape or object that shows how they view the world. Explain to each of them the concept of looking at the world from the eyes of the Avot versus Moshe eyes.

Parashat Va'eira

WAKE UP, CHOOSE RESPONSIBILITY

WHEN WE'RE DEALING with *Sefer Shemot*, entering into the second parashah, it is very clear and obvious that one of the major questions that arises is the question of leadership. What makes a good leader? What makes someone able to elevate people from the lowest to the highest?

One of the definitions we can give is the ability for someone to own up—not for someone to be perfect, and not for somebody to be great. For someone to not be afraid to say to people, "I failed," is what makes a leader incredible. I think if we take this answer, and make an addition that maybe a little different, we can see something miraculous in our parashah.

When Moshe Rabbeinu is described in *perek zayin*, this appears immediately before the description of the lineage of Reuven, followed by Shimon, and then it describes the tribe of Levi until Moshe Rabbeinu and then it stops. If you want to describe Am Yisrael, then go for it! Describe from Reuven all the way down to Binyamin. What is the need to start from Reuven, Shimon, and then Levi? If we think about it on a deep level, we can find an amazing message about the definition of leadership.

Very often, we view leadership as a privilege. We look at it as something that is exalted and something that earns respect. A leader is someone who is greater, who's more talented, who has more ability, who's more special. But that is the antithesis of leadership in Am Yisrael. A leader is not someone that has more ability. A leader is not someone that has more privilege. A leader is someone who is aware of the fact that he does not have privilege, but rather responsibility. Reuven is the first, Shimon is the second, and Levi is the third. Reuven wasn't chosen because of something that he did, and Shimon wasn't chosen for what he couldn't do, so the torch of responsibility went down to Levi. This was saying to Moshe Rabbeinu that he's not getting this torch because he's better, but because he was excited to continue the responsibility that others could not. You are not gaining nor doing something new, and you are not even the first tribe! You are only the extension of the responsibility that others were not blessed to do. When you understand this frame of mind, you no longer see yourself as someone who earns privilege, but as someone who earns responsibility.

So often we stray away from responsibility. We give it to other people, but Moshe Rabbeinu understood that no matter where he went—even if he was in Midyan and saw women being hurt—he needed to take responsibility. What did Moshe get from this? Certainly, there is no privilege in that! Maybe you could say he got a wife afterward, but that's not what he thought would happen. When he went out and saw two people fighting he said to them, "What are you doing?" There was no benefit or privilege for him. There is only toiling and struggling. You look at Moshe Rabbeinu, and he said, "Ribbono Shel Olam, I'm leading the Jewish people and it hurts! It is difficult!" But that is exactly why. It is because you enjoy the opportunity of responsibility. So many *chevreh* around the world ask, "How do you wake up in the morning?" A lot of people have all these ideas of making your bed, putting up your pillow, or having a chocolate bar. All these things are great ideas, but at the end of the day, we all know the only reason that people start off their day is because they recognize responsibility. If they are able to look at themselves and say that I am not waking up because I'm the center, and I am privileged, but it's because I have merited the presence of being responsible.

Moshe Rabbeinu was a person who understood that he wanted responsibility. He didn't need it, but he wanted it. *Moreinu v'Rabbeinu*, Rav Kook, would sign every single letter he would write, "*eved l'am kadosh*." He was excited to be a servant! How many of us are excited to serve? We all go to customer service, but we're not the service. We ask others to serve us, but how excited are we to serve others?

Parashat Bo

PREPARE TO FEEL

> "Ideas take you far away from life;
> practice makes life into an ideal."

OPENING QUESTIONS

1. What would be your first message to a slave being freed from slavery?
2. What are the dangers of redemption?

LEARNING CONVERSATION

It is really essential in this parashah to be aware not only of what happens at the beginning, but also what happens at the end of it.

The parashah begins with the last of the ten *makkot* and ends with the question of "What now?" There had been Ten Plagues and 210 years of slavery, but then what? What is interesting at the end of the parashah is the number of details, even to the extent of addressing what they are going to wear when they leave Mitzrayim, for example.

Could you imagine someone leaving Auschwitz after five years and telling him before he leaves, "I want you to wear a pink shirt." The survivor would probably respond, "Listen, I don't care what I'm wearing; I just want to leave here." Hashem said to Am Yisrael after 210 years, "I want you to have a stick; I want you to have shoes on; and I want you to wear this."

Then Hashem said, "I want to make sure that you take all the matzah." The *Sefat Emet* said in the year 1899, "משארותם צרורות בשמלותם"—They

94

put all of the belongings on them."[1] So, the Midrash asks, "וכי לא הי' להם בהמות—Did they not have animals?"

In other words, why does Hashem tell them, "*You* have to carry the matzot. *You* have to carry the *korban*." They should have just been able to put it all on the animals.

The Midrash answers, "רק לחבב את המצוה—Only so that they should *cherish* the mitzvah." It's not about the act that you are doing, but the feeling that you have while doing it. The reason Hashem told us what to do and what to wear when leaving Mitzrayim is that He wanted to define to us the concept of "What now?" The answer to "What now?" is Am Yisrael's message through the mitzvot. This is our message. This is our consistency. This is our lifestyle—the tefillin we wear, the tzitzit we wear, and the candles we light. All of these things define our religion. Hashem said to Am Yisarel as they left Egypt that the question was "What now?" And the answer was, "You need to understand the secret of the mitzvot."

A mitzvah is not just an action. We tend to get so confused and believe that we are "just" wearing tefillin or that we are "just" reading the Torah, but these are the external expressions of a much greater, life-altering mindset that needs to be taking place. We get so focused on the action, but we need to understand that the answer of *yetziat Mitzrayim* was not to put the mitzvot on your animals, but put them on yourself. Show that you want the mitzvah, and that you are not giving the mitzvah to someone else. Not that you are looking for the easy way, but you are looking for the fun, demanding, and exciting way, by making it part of you. The *Sefat Emet* asks, How can we make sure that the mitzvot we do affect us? A lot of us keep Shabbat, but it doesn't affect us. A lot of us wear tefillin, but it doesn't affect us. A lot of us might even be married, but we don't really feel we're in love. The *Sefat Emet* says the act itself is for Hashem, "אבל הכנת המצוה והתשוקה קודם המצוה ולאחריה—But what will determine if it will affect you is not just the act of the mitzvah but the preparation."

---

1   *Sefat Emet, Bo* 27.

The message of *yetziat Mitzrayim* to Am Yisrael was: I want you to realize it's not about eating the matzah; it's about carrying the matzah. It's not just about keeping Shabbat; it is about preparing for Shabbat. It can't be that Shabbat starts when candle lighting starts. According to the halachot of my wife, Tanya, you shop for Shabbat on Monday. If you wait for Shabbat, you're keeping Shabbat; if you prepare for Shabbat, you want to live Shabbat and feel it.

My berachah, as we enter into the Chodesh of Shevat, is that we should understand and realize that mitzvot are the epicenter of Am Yisrael. The reason that they are so essential is not because of the actions, but from the preparation that they demand of us. We should have the *zechut*, honor, to enjoy practice for basketball games. We should realize that if davening starts at 7:30 and we are not there at 7:29 it means we don't really like it. We should have that opportunity to *le'hitkonein*, prepare, in order to feel, because if we are just there when we have to be there, then we never actually feel the mitzvot.

LIVING THE LEARNING

Choose a mitzvah you feel disconnected from. Make a game plan of how you want to prepare for this mitzvah, and after thirty days of preparing for this mitzvah, see if you feel any different toward the mitzvah.

Parashat Bo

INTERNAL FREEDOM

PARASHAT BO can be called the moment we were waiting for. The exile doesn't seem so long when we read about it in *Sefer Shemot*, but in reality, it was very long. Very long! 210 years of constantly feeling of, "Is it over yet?" But it only continued. The darkness just never seemed to end. Then the moment that we have been waiting for finally comes. The moment we were waiting for is described in something that's called, "*b'Eretz Mitzrayim.*" The Torah emphasizes that Hashem spoke to Moshe and Aharon and revealed to them the message that exile was truly over, and that they were really going out of the darkness. The message was said to them as "*b'Eretz Mitzrayim*" and the obvious question is: Why was there a need to emphasize where they were? We already know! There is no question, and it's not like we thought they were in Africa or in Afghanistan. So, what does this mean that Hashem spoke to them "*b'Eretz Mitzrayim?*" It might teach us that there is a very strong message being given by Hashem.

The message is that Hashem specifically speaks about redemption in the place of darkness and not after. We might have thought, "You know Hashem, get us out, do *makkot bechorot*, and let's speak about redemption later. Let's get out of the misery; let's get out of the pain; let's get to a safer haven, and then in a calmer and healthier environment let's speak about redemption." The message of Hashem is just the opposite of this: He will not wait until afterward! He is actually going to speak to us about the redemption before. It is easy to receive redemption, but the effect of it can be very minute. For example, Hashem comes and redeems you, and then you leave and speak about it five minutes later. There's a chance that the majority of the people stopped feeling it, because feelings end, and they don't last. They may have even been really thankful to Hashem, but they would not have been changed people.

Hashem is not looking to give us the ability to leave; He also wants us to become elevated. The only way to elevate is by changing one's character. Yes, naturally, you don't really believe in redemption until you see it, but Hashem is saying that will not assist you long term. He needed us to sit *"b'Eretz Mitzrayim"* at the same time that the Egyptians were still walking around in your backyards. In the playgrounds, you could see the Egyptian kids playing, but your kids are not allowed to play. In the same place that you've seen everything break, now I need you to recognize that you are the redemption.

If I just take you out, then the redemption is something that is from Egypt, and it will have nothing to do with you. Hashem is saying, "I need Am Yisrael to learn that they are the redemption, they are the solution, and that they are the medicine." They have to sit in their own mirrors and see the same atmosphere and say to themselves, "Although the external is X, the internal is different." That is real freedom. The ability to separate between the external (*Eretz Mitzrayim*) and the internal (*ha'chodesh ha'zeh lachem*). You are sitting *b'Eretz Mitzrayim*, but you are viewing yourselves as new not because the external has changed but because the internal mindset has been elevated. That is true redemption.

The berachah, as we enter into *Parashat Bo*—six weeks before the bar mitzvah of our *bechor*, Ohr Eytan, where the experience of learning for the bar mitzvah has been an incredible moment of education for me and my wife, Tanya, personally to really be able to understand that what we're trying to teach our child—is that we should all become our own redeemers. Just like a bar mitzvah boy learns his own parashah, reading the Torah on his own, wearing his own tefillin, and preparing his own *d'var Torah*. Rav Re'em told Ohr Eytani that he has to write his own *d'var Torah* and not have it written by his parents. This experience of giving the person the freedom to redeem themselves is a great message for the future of Am Yisrael. The message is to not look for an external redeemer, but to ask ourselves what we can do to look at ourselves.

Although the external might be really broken, the internal is something that could shine so strong that it could elevate the brokenness and so that we do not just run away from it.

Parashat Beshalach

EVERLASTING BREAD

> "The only way to raise up the past is to envision the future."

OPENING QUESTIONS

1. Why do you think that immediately after *k'riat Yam Suf* we have a full *perek* teaching about the *mohn*?
2. What is the symbolism of the *mohn* and the bread we eat? How do they create two different paradigms of living?
3. Why is it so important to keep the *mohn* beside the *Aron* for all generations to remember it, if they won't ever eat from it?

LIVING THE LEARNING

On Thursday night do a challah bake with all the kids. Bring to the Shabbat table the best challah from the store and the challah from the challah bake. Ask people to choose which one they would prefer and explain why.

Parashat Beshalach

NESHAMAH

LEARNING CONVERSATION

There's a theme in *Parashat Beshalach* that goes on underneath the surface. We know this parashah is about *kri'at Yam Suf*. But there's a continuing story that goes on throughout the parashah. It says right after they left Mitzrayim that they got to a place and it says, "שם שם לו חק ומשפט—There [God] made for them a statute and an ordinance."[1] *Rashi* says an unusual idea: the moment that they left Mitzrayim, the first mitzvah they received was the mitzvah of Shabbat. Why is it so significant that the moment that they left Egypt they were commanded to keep Shabbat, when we already knew that it was going to be one of the Ten Commandments and it was already part of the Creation of the world? Why now and why here?

That's not the only place that we find this concept of Shabbat. One of the main themes of the *mohn*, the food of the desert, is what happens to it on Shabbat. I think it's very simple to ask ourselves a question, "Why is there such an emphasis on the mitzvah of Shabbat, especially now as they leave Egypt?"

In order to answer that question, I had to think together with the other *rebbeim* in the yeshiva where I teach. Coming into this year in yeshiva, 5779, we had to figure out what *masechta* of Gemara to learn. What Gemara would help the students develop the most during their year in Israel?

---

1   *Shemot* 15:25.

There were many options, but we had to choose a Gemara that's relevant to the past, present, and future of each of the students. We agreed that there's one issue that needed to be addressed immediately: Shabbat. So, we chose to learn *Masechta Shabbat* this year.

How is *Masechta Shabbat* the past, present and future? If you think about what happens when people experience a gap year, they're experiencing a year of no external responsibility. You don't have to make food, earn a salary, or do any work. All you need to do is focus on internal reflection. That's what these students are going through, and therefore *Masechta Shabbat* is the perfect mirror for their gap year.

If you look into the future, anyone who really waits for Shabbat will also change the way they look at all of Judaism. Anyone who leaves yeshiva yearning for the *niggunim*, dancing, food, and *tefillot* of Shabbat will be a different person, no matter where they end up.

How is it connected to the past? Shabbat gives us the ability to continue what happens. For that reason, we chose *Masechta Shabbat*.

Now I will return to *Rashi*'s question. The answer is that the time when they left Egypt was very dangerous. What happens to someone who is unable to achieve anything and suddenly has the opportunity to do everything? He becomes addicted to activity. B'nei Yisrael saw what it meant to be slaves and what it meant to have no freedom. Now they were about to go out of Egypt and change the world. But before they change the world, Hashem gave them Shabbat because if they can't relax, then they can't run a marathon. If you want to learn how to run a marathon, first learn how to breathe.

I'm sitting at a table right now with Avi Karakowsky, who will, *b'ezrat Hashem*, run the entire Jerusalem Marathon. When he's going to be running the whole marathon he has to breathe. Hashem was saying: Am Yisrael, you're going out for a marathon. We're saying to our families: we're going out for a marathon. Let's learn how to breathe. Let's understand that we can enjoy Hashem, and then we can spread our influence.

My berachah to everyone as we enter into *Beshalach*, leaving Egypt and the feeling of slavery, is that we should know that we're able to run the longest marathon in the world if we just know how to breathe.

DEPENDENT REDEMPTION

WE KNOW THE BEGINNING of *Sefer Shemot* deals with exile and the experience of leaving Egypt. But even though we left Egypt, Egypt didn't leave us. We needed the story of *Yam Suf* to not only leave the place, but also leave the people, the culture, and the mindset. It is interesting to pay attention to the things that happen right after the story of *k'riat Yam Suf*. After *k'riat Yam Suf* we were really able to release ourselves from the people, the culture, and the mindset of Egypt, but immediately after we learn about the story of the *mohn* (manna) and we learn about this special food that came from *Shamayim*. It is very important to think what is the message that Hashem was giving the Jewish people by immediately following their redemption with the giving of the *mohn*?

To understand the *mohn* in a little bit of a deeper level, *Moreinu v'Rabbeinu* Rav Kook explains in his *Siddur Olat Re'iyah* that there are two types of sustenance that Hashem gives us directly from the sky. One of them was the *mohn*, the food that we speak about in this parashah, which is the bread of delicacy that comes directly from *Shamayim* to the world, while the second thing that Hashem gives the Jewish people and the world is the rain which is also a direct sustenance. Rav Kook explains the difference between the *mohn* and *mayim*, water—since they both come down directly from the sky—on a more Chassidic level. The word *mohn* is comprised of two letters, *mem*, מ which has a numerical value of forty and *nun*, נ, which has a numerical value of fifty, together being ninety. *Mayim* is composed of three letters; *mem*, מ, which is forty *yud*, י, which is ten, and another *mem*, מ, which is forty, giving us a total of ninety as well. This shows us that they both have the same *gematria*. So, what is the difference between them?

When we think about the *mohn*, it's called *"chessed,"* kindness, meaning that it comes directly from the sky, and it needs zero involvement from human beings. Hashem brings it to the world, and you put it into your mouth. There is no processing, no building, no changing, no adding, no salt, and no pepper. It just comes down, you put it into your mouth, and everything is good.

The water is something that is also amazing, and it enables all the living creatures of the world to survive, but it's something that in order for man to get enjoyment from it, there needs to be some sort of process. Rain on its own will not give us sustenance. We need to first build a pit, receive the water, bring the water out, and then purify it, and only then can we drink it. There is a lot that man needs to do with the water before he can drink it. Rav Kook explains that this is why, in the davening, we say *gevurot geshamim* because rain is obviously *chessed*, but the way it's presented is through *gevurah*, judgment. It's presented as limited, as if Hashem were not giving us with His full hand. He is giving us the ability, but He is not giving us the end; He is not giving us the conclusion, and He is not giving us the result. He is leaving that all up to us.

The first food that Hashem gives Am Yisrael immediately after *Yam Suf* is specifically not *mayim*, but rather *mohn*. The *mohn* is saying that before man learns about his abilities, before he becomes involved, before he changes things, the greatest present for a nation that's beginning their journey is to learn that they are dependent. They are dependent on Hashem and therefore also dependent on one another. They are dependent on not taking too much of the *mohn*, because if you took too much then someone else won't have enough. Therefore, the first food that Hashem gave was different from the water, because He was saying that before you become independent, before you learn about your ability to change, develop, help, and assist, recognize that you are dependent.

The message that Hashem is giving us as we go into the story of redemption is that if you want something to last then you are not allowed to think of it independently. If you want something strong, recognizing independence is so important. If you want something exalted, then learn—learn about your ability to change and develop. If you are looking for something that will make things last long-term for everyone, then learn about the beauty of being dependent.

B'ezrat Hashem we are hopefully nearing the end of the COVID-19 pandemic. One of the things that is going to happen, *b'ezrat Hashem*, is that we are going to become very independent again. We are going to fly all over the world, we are going to make all the things that we used to do, we are going to have the ability to plan things and not have everything be canceled because this happened, and this happened, and this happened. Over the last year, we learned how dependent we are on one another, for when someone is in isolation, they can't even take out their own garbage. This is what it's like to live in a world where you are dependent. Obviously, we prefer to learn all this from the *mohn* instead, but one of the things that we can develop within ourselves is the beauty and the blessing of learning that it's not weak to be dependent on people. It means that we are aware that we're not trying to worship ourselves.

I give us all the berachah as we go into *Parashat Beshalach*, the story of redemption, that we should be redeemed from the coronavirus and that we should learn that the language that we need to learn should be linked to the past and to being aware of the future, and that these should be linked to each other. We should not constantly be separated all the time in our own boxes and forget about the beautiful circle that we can be a part of.

Parashat Yitro

LEARN, DON'T SOLVE

> "Learning problems instead of solving problems may be a slower fix, but it is more efficient in the long run."

OPENING QUESTIONS

1. What caused Am Yisrael to fail with the *chet ha'egel* immediately after the special moment of *maamad Har Sinai*?
2. What was unique or special about Har Sinai?
3. If Am Yisrael failed right after Har Sinai, then what was the point of Har Sinai?

LEARNING CONVERSATION

In *Parashat Yitro*, we get to *maamad Har Sinai*. There are many questions that we could deal with there, but the question that I want to address this week is the question of, "What was the point?" A lot of us know that *maamad Har Sinai* was followed by the *chet ha'egel*. So as great as it was and as special as it was, a moment later it almost all evaporated. So, if this is what happened, then we have to ask: What is the point?

The *Sefat Emet*, in the year 1892, spoke about the significance of *maamad Har Sinai*. The *pasuk* reads, "יום אשר עמדת‎—a day that you stood."[1] The *pasuk* explains that *maamad Har Sinai* was special because we *stood* in front of Hashem. The *Sefat Emet* wants to understand what is the

---

1   *Devarim* 4:10.

meaning of *amadeta*? And how does that define the significance of Har Sinai? He says, "כי בהר סיני באו בנ"י לתכלית השלימות. והיו כמלאכים".[2] The *Sefat Emet* explains there are two words that describe the difference between men and angels. The definition of man is that he is a *mehalach*, moving. The idea is that we are constantly changing. We go up, and then we go down. Things go well, and then they go wrong. The angles are defined as *omdim*, standing. The *pasuk* says that what happened at *maamad Har Sinai* is that Am Yisrael was transformed from a state of *mehalach*, moving, into a state of *omdim*, standing and being. We suddenly became not human, but angels.

How does this help us understand the question that we started with? The question was: What is the point of *maamad Har Sinai* if right afterward there was the *chet ha'egel*? I think the *Sefat Emet* is teaching that what happened at *maamad Har Sinai* is that it showed us the tools. It didn't give us the solutions, and it didn't say that things were going to be perfect, but it did give us the tools. It gave us the tools to know that internally we are angels. We might continue our lives, and we might fall right after. There is always the possibility for the concept of the *chet ha'egel*. At the end of the day, we have to realize that at the beginning, with the establishment, and at the core of our existence, we are like angels. *Maamad Har Sinai* is so important because we were like angels. How can we overcome the *chet ha'egel* in our own lives? How can we deal with all the misfortunes and things that don't work out? The answer is that if all you are trying to do is solve whatever went wrong, then you are always going to look for something minor. However, if you feel like you are an angel, then you'll realize that sometimes the solution could be major. Not solving the minor mistake, but rather learning from the mistake, is a major concept that shows us how we are angelic and capable of the impossible sometimes.

I had the privilege today of speaking to a student, a senior in high school. I asked him, "For you, What is your goal of going to Israel for the year?" He responded back to me, "I know that there are going to

---

2   *Sefat Emet, Yitro,* 20.

be times in my life that I will be in places where there is no inspiration, and I want to be able to get to a level where I have the ability to deal with those obstacles." This is exactly the concept of *maamad Har Sinai:* because it is not unaware of the challenge, but rather is aware of the challenge. It's not trying to create an alternative by saying choose Har Sinai or the *chet ha'egel*. Rather it is saying that Har Sinai gives us an awareness of ways that we can deal with the *chet ha'egel*—not by think-ing that the *chet ha'egel* is simple, but by realizing that we have received tools that don't just give us the memory of the special moments but give us the vision of what it means to deal with difficulties and challenges.

Rav Kook describes that the idea of *tefillah* is "להוציא מהכוח אל הפועל." He means that the idea and the experience of *tefillah* is not just the experience of saying the words, but it's about knowing that in the idea of *tefillah*, there is this concept of potential. When we are asking for a *refuah*—health, or *parnasah*—wealth, or *geshem*—rain, we are really just saying that we have all these things in potential, but we want them to be revealed through *tefillah*. *Maamad Har Sinai* showed us the poten-tial and the strength. Then immediately afterward, we need to realize that although we were in that space, it's not about the memory of that space, but it's about how that redefines who you are. From now on you are not just a *mehalach*—mover, but you are no different than angels. If you view yourself like an angel, and you see yourself like an angel, then the way you will deal with your challenges will be different. You are not only going to solve your problems, but you will learn from them. Your perspective and understanding of the *chet ha'egel* will be very different if before that you were an angel.

When my wife, Tanya, gets the opportunity to speak to our children, she often speaks to them not just about what they didn't do, but about the concept of them as being almost perfect. If you see a parent who sees their child as perfect, then the child understands themselves dif-ferently, and their way of dealing with things is not just to overcome, but to grow. We can learn this all from *maamad Har Sinai*.

My berachah as we enter *Parashat Yitro* and we listen again to *maamad Har Sinai* is that we should realize that the real significance of it was not that we weren't going to fail, but that it gave us the tools and ways to deal with failure. Not just as a solution, but as an opportunity for learning different ways of growing from the challenges we have after *maamad Har Sinai*, through the perfect and angelic experience of *maamad Har Sinai*.

LIVING THE LEARNING

Write on a piece of paper twenty words the describe your family. Give everyone at the Shabbat table twenty seconds to look at it, and then have them compete over who remembers as many of the twenty words as they can.

Parashat Yitro

A HAPPENING TORAH

THE FAMOUS QUESTION that all of us ask on *Parashat Yitro* is: Why is the introduction to *Matan Torah* Yitro telling Moshe Rabbeinu how to implement the court system of Am Yisrael?

We know that *Matan Torah* is found in *perek yud-tet*. In *Perek yud-chet* Yitro tells Moshe Rabbeinu that he must not run the court system alone and that he needs to have others helping him. Why is this the introduction to *Matan Torah*?

When we think about Yitro, we will find that there is something unique about him. Yitro had many different names. *Rashi* teaches us, according to the Midrash, that Yitro had seven different names. We see a few of them in the Torah, and a few in the Midrash, but overall, he had seven different names. What does it mean that an individual has seven names? On the most basic level, a name is the identity of a person. If a person has seven names, they can therefore change their identity multiple times. Not once, not twice, but they constantly change themselves.

Maybe Yitro, as an individual who was willing to be the first convert, was willing to change and challenge himself. Yitro was willing to leave his comfort zone from where he was living in Midyan and go all the way to the desert. This character, who understands the idea of change, is the introduction to the giving of the Torah. The idea of the Torah is that it was not something that was just given. Instead, it is something that is being given. It is something that is constantly transforming and changing in the way that people relate to it.

In *Masechta Chagigah*, Rabbi Yehoshua asks his students, "מה חידוש היה בבית המדרש היום—What new idea was there in the *beit midrash*

110

today?"[1] *Mori v'rabi*, Rav Re'em, asked, "Why is this the question he asks?" Rav Re'em answered that he asks this because it is the definition of learning Torah; *Chiddush*—something that it is being revived, renewed. We are not trying to reminisce over what happened. Instead, we have to be aware that it is happening, and that we are involved, and that we are not just receivers. Therefore, for the introduction to *Matan Torah* we have Yitro—a person who recognized that in order to have the ability to relate to the Torah, you must be able to internalize the fact that the Torah is not static. The Torah is not something that ended or is merely from the past. The Torah is something that is happening; it is relevant, and it needs our interpretation and involvement.

Maybe that is also what Yitro was saying to Moshe. Moshe came out of Egypt as the one leader, the one that everyone turned to. Yitro was saying to Moshe, "You need to develop, be aware, transform, and to really teach the nation. It is true that maybe for yourself you can be the one judge, but this won't work in the future. No one will be like you, Moshe. No single person can be a lone judge. If you want to be someone that can make the Torah relevant, do not just do what you need, Moshe, do what they will need in the future, so it can continue and develop."

My berachah when we walk into the parashah of *Matan Torah* is that we should realize and understand that our *Sefer Torah* is an *eitz chaim*, a tree of life. It is alive, relevant, and speaking to us. The Torah is giving us new life all the time. We cannot look at the Torah as a book from the past, that has ended, and will not renew itself. This is why *Parashat Yitro* is the "introduction" to *Matan Torah*. This is why Moshe's developing a court system—which shows an awareness of what will be needed in the future, is the only way to realize the purpose of learning Torah and the goal of receiving the Torah from Hashem.

---

1   *Chagigah* 3a.

FRAME FIRST

"Tension isn't asking for a decision of hierarchy (one is better than the other), but rather is demanding a relationship between the different pieces."

OPENING QUESTIONS

1. Why are the details of *Parashat Mishpatim* immediately after Har Sinai?
2. Why is the selling of a slave the first issue succeeding the exalted high of *Aseret Hadibrot*?
3. What should be the right balance between the *neshamah* and the *guf* that each of us deal with on a daily basis?

LIVING THE LEARNING

Build a hundred-piece puzzle. First make the frame and then add the middle pieces. Try to experience the frame as the *guf* that makes room for the creative middle *neshamah* pieces to shine.

BRING IT HOME

PARASHAT MISHPATIM is best understood if we compare it to the parashah before, namely *Yitro*. On a very basic level, they appear to be total opposites. If you think about *Parashat Yitro*, it is very general. There are not a lot of details oriented toward *maamad Har Sinai*; Hashem says very big, general things. It is very experiential: there is fire and lightning, Am Yisrael is screaming, Hashem is "yelling," and Moshe is running. It is a parashah that is filled with energy, excitement, and experience. On a very general level, it addresses the relationship between God and man. You go into *Parashat Mishpatim*, and it is one of the most detailed parshiyot in the entire Torah. It goes into the most minuscule details. You are dealing with total opposites. *Parashat Mishpatim* deals with the most mundane, normal, regular, day-to-day experiences. Yet these two parshiyot are right next to each other. We might think that Hashem would give us some kind of a separation. Why are they so close?

But the question gets so much bigger. Not only are they so close, but the first letter of *Parashat Mishpatim* makes this connection even stronger. The letter between *Parashat Mishpatim* and *Parashat Yitro* is the letter "*vav*." *Rashi* explains that anywhere in the Torah where it says the word *eileh*, it is to separate, whereas if it says the word *v'eileh*, the connotation is to relate and connect. When I was learning this *Rashi*, I asked myself why it was specifically here that *Rashi* brings this explanation. Based on what we said before, it is because we would have expected *eileh*. It seems like these two parshiyot are different and that it should have said "*eileh hamishpatim*." *Parashat Yitro* is dealing with the big excitement, and *Parashat Mishpatim* is dealing with the details.

Comes this parashah and says *v'eileh*, I am connecting these two opposites. The question is why?

Oftentimes, we build theories and have visions and dreams. This is *Parashat Yitro*. The problem with all of our dreams is that we do not make a game plan. So many people speak about making family their ideal. You need to ask them the *Mishpatim* question: What is your game plan? A lot of people speak about the greatness of having a relationship with God, but what is the game plan? When are you waking up every day? What and when are you learning? A lot of people love to learn *Chassidut* and Kabbalah, which is very much linked to *Parashat Yitro*. But are you really able to learn halachah? One needs to be aware that Yitro is needed, but it needs to give one the stamina to build the game plan. The experiences are so needed and so special, but on condition that you are willing to locate them, bring them down, and relate them to a game plan.

My berachah to all of us entering *Parashat Mishpatim* is that we should all have vision, experiences, and moments of inspiration. However, if we do not focus on how to transform theory into practice, our theories are not only unactualized, but they can actually become dangerous. They become removed from reality.

WHO IS AMALEK?

WE ALL KNOW the concept that thirty days before any holiday we have to start dealing with the holiday. The idea of this halachah is two-fold. Firstly, you will only connect to a holiday through the preparation for it. The only way to have a holiday really affect us is not by experiencing it when it is, but by starting it before and therefore recognizing that only through the preparation will the holiday be internalized. The second side of this concept is that although maybe the day itself is on a certain date, the effect of it is much bigger. Even though Purim is not a month away, but three weeks away, we have to enter into the depth of what Purim is about in order for us to really experience the redemption from Haman. The first question that we want to develop is the story of Amalek. There is no way to enter into the story of Purim without analyzing Amalek. The question is: Why? Why is it so important to understand Amalek? The answer is that it's strongly emphasized that Haman was "*Agagi*," meaning that he was the descendant of Agag, the King of Amalek. The idea of the Megillah and the hatred that Haman had was that it did not begin with Haman. It all began in *Sefer Shemot* with the war against Amalek. The simple question to ask when the Torah describes, "ויבא עמלק וילחם עם ישראל ברפידם—Amalek came and fought with Israel at Refidim," is: Why is there no explanation?[1] Meaning, what in the world were they looking for? We did not even have the Torah yet, so if they wanted to fight against our religion, this didn't apply to us because it wasn't defined yet. We were in the desert because we

---

1   *Shemot* 17:8.

didn't have a country, so if they were fighting the idea of the message of the Land of Israel, it wasn't yet a thing because we didn't have a land. We were a bunch of slaves walking through a desert and that bothered them so much. So, our question is, Why did they come against us?

There are many answers to what the motivation for Amalek was for fighting against the Jewish people, but one of the options is to look at the *pasuk* right before the war with Amalek. Am Yisrael said to Moshe, "היש י-הוה בקרבנו אם אין"—Is God present among us or not?"[2] The *pasuk* that introduces Amalek is a question the Jewish people were asking which is, "Is Hashem with us?" They were not asking if there is a God or not, because the day before they were at *Yam Suf*! They saw the ocean split! They saw frogs jump out of jugs! They saw blood turn into water and water turn into blood! And they saw darkness in one area that wasn't in another area! There was no question in their minds if there was a God, but there was a question of what is the relevance of Hashem to us? Okay so we understand that there is a God, but what does that mean that He is part of me? I'm just a random guy in the world, I don't have a Torah, there are no mitzvot that have been given, so I don't really know if I have a connection? Is God in us?

Amalek comes as a result of maybe the most important issue: a lack of confidence. The question that the Jewish people are asking is, "I know that there can be a great experience, I know that there can be a great God, I know that there could be a great redemption, but does that mean that when I'm looking in the mirror that I see a different person? Should I look at myself as a having different potential? Should I see myself as being renewed by the new revelation or is the new revelation something beyond?" Amalek understood that the only thing that they needed to fight for was clarity. The moment that someone clearly understands that not only is there a God, but that they were chosen by God, then you cannot stop that person.

We know the famous story of a Chassidic Rebbe, the *Baal HaTanya*, who was in jail when someone walked in and puts a gun to his head. The

---

2   *Shemot* 17:7.

man told him, "Rebbe, I'm going to shoot you," and the *Baal HaTanya*
sat there and smiled. The policeman looked at the *Baal HaTanya* and he
was like, "I don't get it. I have a gun and you don't. Why are you smiling?
I should be the one smiling." The *Baal HaTanya* responded, "If you have
one world, then you're right that a gun controls a person. But when you
have two worlds, your gun is just my key into the next."

When someone really believes that God is within them, then there
is no stopping them and Amalek understands this. They realized that
if Am Yisrael fully understood that God was within them, there would
be no stopping these people forever. There is no stopping something
infinite no matter how finite you want to be. It could be with guns,
with gas, or with war. You could do whatever you want, but it's finite.
The moment that a person sees themselves as infinite, there is no way
that you can ever stop them. Therefore, Amalek was scared of our confidence; They were scared of our clarity, and they were scared of us not
doubting ourselves. The only thing that Amalek said is, "Are you sure?"

Am Yisrael was so excited and all Amalek had to say is, "Are you sure?
Are you sure that God chose you? Do you have proof? Give me a document, give me a Torah—are you sure? Prove it." Those are the scariest
two questions you can ever ask a person who's connected to something
infinite, because you can't prove it. Something infinite is not something
that is without doubt, because there is a tension within a person who
is finite who believes in God who is infinite. Since you are finite, you
think to yourself, "Maybe God doesn't care. Maybe God doesn't like me.
Maybe He's not there." There is nothing obvious! God doesn't speak
to us on a daily basis, and so Amalek tunes into this doubt and tunes
into this lack of confidence. And what is our reaction to Amalek? Our
reaction to Amalek is, "You're right. I have no proof. Therefore, I am
going to fight for it forever."

If you go over to a person and ask, "Are you sure you chose the right
profession?" They're not. If you go over to a person and ask, "Are you
sure you chose the right spouse?" There is no way to prove it. In the
things that there is so much doubt, there is also so much potential for
work. That is the greatest God gives us if we really understand how
to fight against Amalek. Amalek sees the doubt. They see the problem

between the finite and infinite, and they say: If there's doubt then the game is over, and God doesn't love you. Yet we say the opposite, because by saying there's doubt, it means that God believes in us. It means that God is saying: I believe in you! Wherever there is clarity, there's no need for work. Whenever something is obvious or wherever anything is 100 percent, then the game is over. Am Yisrael needs to say to Amalek, "It's not obvious. Our world is torn; there is doubt; there is no clarity; and therefore, I am going to get involved. I am going to be more creative. I am going to find more and more answers for how to deal with the deepest question that Amalek is asking us, which is: "Are you sure that God is in you?"

Baruch Hashem, this Friday we're going into Rosh Chodesh Adar and Ohr Eytan is going to put on his tefillin for the first time. If you saw the excitement that he had when he was putting on his tefillin, you'd be like, "Oh my God, this love will never be extinguished." But someone a little bit older might say to him when he's putting his tefillin on, "Ohr Eytan, in another year or two you're not going to feel the same way." Ohr Eytan would respond by saying, "That's an Amalek sentence." It's true you are not going to feel that way in two years, but that doesn't scare me, it excites me. It excites me that I don't have God saying to me every second, "Here's the obvious answer," because it means that I need to make the answer. It means that God believes in me and therefore He creates the doubt for me.

Parashat Terumah

TORAH FOR ALL

L'Iluy nishmat Eitan Eliezer ben Mordechai, on Ethan's first yahrzeit.

B'EZRAT HASHEM we will connect the idea of this parashah to *mori v'rabi*, Reb Ethan, who passed away a year ago. When we enter into *Parashat Terumah*, we enter into the *Mishkan*. For most of us today, the *Mishkan* is very distant and removed, and it does not have so much relevance to our lives. What we do not realize, however, is that maybe the *Mishkan* is a miniature image of the perfect world. It gives us not only vessels but also messages. To understand one of the messages of the *Mishkan*, I would like to learn the opening word for each *pasuk* describing the commands to build three different vessels that we learn about in *perek chaf-gimmel*. When we read about the *Shulchan* it says "וְעָשִׂיתָ שֻׁלְחָן—You shall make a table."[1] When it talks about the *Menorah* it says, "וְעָשִׂיתָ מְנֹרַת זָהָב טָהוֹר—You shall make a *Menorah* of pure gold."[2] There is only one vessel in the *Mishkan* whose description starts differently, and that is the *Aron*. The *Aron* starts off with a word that is similar but different. It says "וְעָשׂוּ אֲרוֹן עֲצֵי שִׁטִּים—They shall make an Ark of acacia wood."[3] *V'asu* is the same action as *v'asita* which means acting or building, but is plural. A major question is why the commands to build the *Menorah* and *Shulchan* are addressed in singular while the *Aron* is addressed in plural.

There are many answers—one of which is that actively, the *Aron*, *Menorah*, and *Shulchan* would be built by one person, yet there is a very clear distinction between the *Aron* and the other vessels. The other

---

1 *Shemot* 25:23.
2 *Shemot* 25:31.
3 *Shemot* 25:10.

vessels deal with specific things. The lights of the *Menorah* deal with spirituality. The *Shulchan* deals with physicality. The concept of the building of the *kli*, vessel, is that it cannot start by *v'asita*; it is not singular, not individual. The Torah needs and must be relevant to everything, everyone, everywhere. The Torah is not a subject, a topic. Instead, it is something that gives you a lens on everything and everyone, with a different perspective.

I met Ethan four years ago. I used to think that there are people who could basically only do one thing. When I met Ethan, I met someone who could lift weights, learn Torah, care for children, and excel in *kibbud horim*, someone who could relate to his grandparents and understand who all of these things are interconnected. When I walked into the first yahrzeit of Ethan, it was obvious and clear to me that he had been the image of a walking *Aron*—a person who realized that it wasn't OK to make Torah something judgmental, something that only related to a certain group of people. Torah needs to be something that relates to five-year-olds and ninety-year-olds. If it is not, then it is not a real Torah.

CELEBRATE DOUBT

STARTING THE SECOND PART of our entrance into Purim, it's very important, as we spoke about earlier, to really understand Amalek and the war against them. There's one appearance that I think if we go deeper into, we'll realize something tremendous about the war that we have against Amalek. We know that Amalek, עמלק, has a *gematria* of 240 and the word for doubt, ספק, is also 240. Although numbers sometimes seem to be a nice additional game, with regards to Amalek it is definitional—understanding that Amalek is all about doubt and trying to create more doubt by moving into places of doubt. We see that when Am Yisrael was in the desert and in a place that was very nerve-wracking, where there was no army, no confidence, and they had no country—that is where Amalek attacks: In the place of doubt. Similarly, in the story of Esther, we were in exile; we had nothing they could gain from us—no army, no country— but that is when they attacked: when there was a place of doubt.

We know that the words that appear by Amalek, "אשר קרך בדרך," meaning that they were undeterred by fear of God, also appear in the Megillah regarding Haman.[1] The word *karcha* seems to be only connected to Amalek. *Rashi* wants to understand what this word is teaching us about Amalek, and he explains three different approaches for us:

1. *Karcha* could come from the word *kar* meaning cold. When you're in doubt, you are cold and you're not passionate, nor do you have clarity.
2. *Karcha* could come from the word *mikreh*, when you feel everything is a coincidence. Even if you are successful, who says it will

---

1   *Devarim* 25:18.

stay that way? So, there is a lot of doubt connected to the word *mikreh*.

3. *Karcha* could come from the word *keri*, representing *tum'ah*. This makes us very unconfident about our future and our destiny and suggests that maybe we're impure and maybe we're not going to succeed.

We see that this numerical connection is much greater than just a number, and it's really the essence and the core of what Amalek is about. We could also see this in the way that Haman tried to kill us. He was the first one to throw lots, and obviously his lottery was significant because it is the reason for the name of the holiday. Haman was showing that not only was he planning to kill us, but that he was going to kill us through "coincidence." Amalek is very strong on this concept of "lotteries," and if we look closely, we can see something very unique about the war with them. We said that Amalek emphasizes doubt and the things that are unclear, but the scariest thing is that on the holiest day of our year, Yom Kippur—whose name is very similar to the word "Purim"—we also cast lots. So, when we see Haman casting lots we say, "Wow, Amalek is so bad!" But we ourselves also cast lots! So, if Amalek is so wrong, then why do we do the same thing?

In fact, it's not only with the lotteries where we see a comparison to Amalek and where we fight Amalek with his own medicine. One example is that Haman wanted to hang Mordechai on a tree, but we ended up hanging Haman on that very same tree! We fed him his own medicine! We attacked him with his own remedy!

Another example appears during the celebration that Achashverosh held when Esther decided that she wanted to fight against Haman. Here too, she used that same remedy of "*mishteh*." She used that same concept from the beginning of the Megillah of throwing parties.

Furthermore, we see the same thing with the horse. The horse that Haman thought would be used for him, ended up going to Mordechai!

We know the war against Amalek also said, "כי יד על כס י-ה—Hand upon the throne of the God!"[2] Amalek put their hands on the chair of

---

2   *Shemot* 17:16.

Hashem. So how did we fight back against Amalek? With the hands of Moshe Rabbeinu! As scary as Amalek seems, we do the same things! They fought with their hands, so Moshe fought back with his hands. They built a tree, and we fought back with a tree. They wanted a horse, and we fought back with a horse. They threw a party, and we too threw a party. I think with this appearance we could learn a tremendous idea about Amalek: They are right! Amalek is right that the idea of doubt is not something which is made up—it's true.

At Har Sinai, there was clarity, and without that experience there would be no clarity. We live in a world where nothing is clear and everything is full of doubt, and Amalek is right that we do not know the future. There is no document that says that Am Yisrael will stay in Israel forever from 1948. There's no clarity, and no one promised it, so there is a very serious doubt of whether we will stay. The more important something is, the less we can prove it. We are telling Amalek that they are right, and we agree with you, but our conclusions are very different. Amalek's conclusion is that nothing matters and that everything is a joke. Almost like the Joker from Batman—maybe he's like the image of Haman, that if there's doubt or unclarity, then let's laugh at life—not laugh with life, not have laughter in life, not enjoy life, but have the mindset that nothing matters. If there's no clarity, then everything's random and nothing matters. We acknowledge to Amalek that this is all true, but our conclusions are very different. Because there is doubt, we need to create clarity. No one can promise someone under their chuppah that it's going to last forever. No one can tell someone when they choose a job that they made the right choice. No one can tell someone when they choose a certain school that it's going to be the right one. Therefore, our conclusion is that this is what makes you responsible and makes you involved. The doubts are what make us participate.

I don't know where my son, Ohr Eytan, is going to be as he's entering his bar mitzvah in two weeks. Do I know what he's going to be like when he's eighteen? I don't! This doesn't mean that I don't care; it means that I care more. I need to get involved even more. I need to participate even more. I need to care even more. The doubt is an opportunity, and not a problem. The doubt is what makes us part of the picture; it doesn't destroy the picture. I think this is what we see with Amalek. They attacked us with the tree, and we attack them with the tree. They cast lots, and we cast lots. If they bring out a horse, then we'll bring out a horse. If they throw a party, we'll throw a party. Our conclusion, however, is different.

In *Masechta Megillah* it teaches that at Achashverosh's party they celebrated by speaking about the beauty of women. They would say Maday is prettier; Peras is prettier; the women of Casdin women are prettier. How is our party different? We do not praise the nothingness; but rather, we say *divrei Torah*! So, what is the Gemara teaching? At their party they were celebrating the external nothingness while we're creating an internal demand. We have to recognize that the party was an opportunity to get involved more deeply into the picture. There's no guarantee if we're going to be in the Land of Israel forever, and therefore we need to join the army, we need to fight, we need to build yeshivot, we need to build our families, and we need to plant trees. Israel doesn't give answers—it makes demands and that's similar to the celebration of Purim. It is recognizing the reality which is doubt. Doubt is not something to be afraid of; it's something to realize that it's causing us to not let go but to hold on. It doesn't just let us see things as a free fall, but as something that's asking us to put our signature on. And that is what will get us more excited for the celebration of life.

DON'T JUST PREVENT

LEARNING CONVERSATION

We're entering into the second parashah about the *Mishkan*, and one of the things that stands out so clearly about the *Mishkan* is how organized it was. The Torah lists each of the *keilim* one by one in great detail. The Torah starts from inside the *Kodesh Hakodashim* (the *Aron*), and then it describes the outer *Mizbei'ach*, the *Shulchan*, and the *Menorah*. So, it specifies vessels of the *Mishkan* based on their location, progressing from inside to the outside. There's a problem, though. There's one missing vessel, the inner *Mizbei'ach*, the *Mizbei'ach Ha'ketoret*, the incense Altar. You'll find it at the end of *Parashat Tetzaveh*.

So, the *Ramban* and *Rashi* ask why this is the case. Why is the *Mizbei'ach Ha'ketoret*, which should have been listed together with the *Shulchan* and the *Menorah* removed? Why is it described all by itself?

The *Ramban* has an amazing, profound, and transformative answer. He says that you have to understand that in life there are two goals. One of them is to remove problems and another one is called to create new light.

According to the *Ramban*, the entire *Mishkan* is a reaction to the most painful experience—or one of the most painful experiences—in Jewish history. The *chet ha'egel*, the Sin of the Golden Calf, took place when we had everything, and then we lost it all. Right after he had been so completely unified with Hashem, Moshe took the *Luchot* and shattered them. By shattering them, he understood that the whole relationship was broken. Obviously, they would rebuild, but Moshe needed the nation to recognize what a low level they had reached. The *Mishkan* was a reaction to that event. Everything about the *Mishkan* centered around

125

rebuilding. How could they remove the pain? How could they return back to Hashem?

From that standpoint, the *Mishkan* was a way to repair the problem of a broken relationship. But they still had to create a new light. That's where the incense Altar comes in. The inner *Mizbei'ach* was giving a new message to the to the *Mishkan*, a message that wasn't about the *chet ha'egel* or about the problem of their broken relationship. The *chet ha'egel* taught us that fixing a broken relationship is not enough. The *Aron* fixed that; the *Menorah* fixed that; the *Shulchan* fixed that, and the outer *Mizbei'ach* fixed that (another *shiur* for another time). The *Rambam* says that the inner *Mizbei'ach* wasn't lumped with the other vessels because it had a different purpose. And the goal of the inner *Mizbei'ach* was linked to the idea of the incense.

If you look back at the first sin of Adam HaRishon in Gan Eden, all of his senses took part in the sin. He saw the tree, he heard his wife, and he tasted the fruit. But the only sense that doesn't participate in the sin is the nose, because *reyach*, smell, is like the word *ruach*, spirit, and can never ever be touched by sin. What's the idea of the *Mizbei'ach Ha'ketoret*? It's there to remind you that although Hashem was happy that B'nei Yisrael were fixing their problems, they needed to go one step further. They also need to make a mission statement.

We're sitting in a room with two incredible people. One of them is one of the greatest leaders of the Jewish people, Josh Greenwald. I'm sitting in an airport, and I just got a text message from him that said, "I'm working on my mission statement." That's what the inner *Mizbei'ach* teaches us: that I'm working, and it takes time, and it takes effort. Also, right next to me is Jonah Lasko. Jonah is not a basketball player; he's a basketball captain. To be a basketball player you need to play defense and you need to score some points. But to be a captain, you need to create a mission for your team. You need to have a vision of where you want your team to go.

The *Mizbei'ach Ha'ketoret* is out of order because we finished the *Mishkan*. We dealt with the pain of the *chet ha'egel*. Now we have to reconstruct our relationship.

So many of us get involved with our children, but not in the right way. We get upset when their rooms aren't clean or when they didn't do well on a test. But when was the last time that we went out for coffee with our children? When was the last time we really tried to develop our relationship with them? A relationship with a child can't be based on their performance, or they'll just turn into robots. Our children are precious, and we need to commit to building a strong relationship with them. I think that's what the *Mizbei'ach Ha'ketoret* is teaching us, that sometimes we need to stop fixing the problem and start building a new light. Being a parent isn't about correcting mistakes or disciplining; it's about nurturing the leaders of the future.

I give us a berachah as we enter into the second parashah of the *Mishkan*, that we should realize that there are many problems in the world that we need to fix, but sometimes in order to actually fix the world we need to build a new mission statement first.

PURIM. PURIM. PURIM.

B'EZRAT HASHEM, we all know that we are entering into *Parashat Tetzaveh*. We are entering into Purim, and the question all the *chevrah* are asking themselves, deep deep in their *neshamot*, is what is the connection between *Parashat Tetzaveh* and Purim?

We know that *Parashat Tetzaveh* can be summarized, *b'etzem*, essentially, in one word: clothing. We have an entire parashah teaching us about the *eiphod*, the Kohen's garment, the *choshen*, the Kohen's breastplate, and the *tzitz*, the Kohen's headpiece; the entire parashah deals with clothing. We have to take one step back and think about the relevance. Really, who cares? I understand that you need the *Mishkan*, but if you wore a colored shirt, would this really matter? Does the color, material, size, and way the clothing was made matter? I do not think any of us are involved in making clothing right now, and not a lot of people care about these details, so we are going into *Parashat Tetzaveh* with the biggest question: Why is there an entire parashah dealing with clothing?

Maybe what we are trying to teach the world is that we do not actually know what clothing is. Rav Nachman from Breslov teaches that most of us think clothing is a presentation for others; we put on a suit to show to other people that we are getting married or working. We wear all these clothes to present ourselves to others. Rav Nachman says that this does not make any sense, because the halachah says that a *talmid chacham* who has a garment with a *pegam*, a blemish or stain on it, is *chayav mitah*, liable for the death penalty. Why in the world would a *talmid chacham* with a little *pegam* on his clothing be *chayav mitah*? Rav Nachman answers that the clothing is a presentation not to the world, but to ourselves. The clothing you wear is how you perceive yourself, how you want to identify yourself, and who and what you are. They are an understanding of what you are. Therefore, when a Kohen wears a *tzitz*, it is not so that other will see. Instead, it is because it gives him the mindset of who he is. Similarly, when a Jew looks in the mirror, sees he is wearing tzitzit, and he is walking next to the turtle at the University of Maryland, he says to himself that this is who he is, a Jew. When he walks around and wears a certain shirt that says "Burgers Bar" on it, he knows who he works for; he knows a piece of his identity, who he is searching for, and what his vision is.

So, Rav Nachman teaches us that the whole idea of *Parashat Tetzaveh* is that we have to redefine clothing not as something that is going outward, but rather, as something that is going inward. We wear it because it is who we want to be. This is the introduction into the idea of costumes on Purim. The costumes make us realize not that we are making a joke out of ourselves, and not that we should wear costumes that make us look like fools, but rather that they show us an image of who we are looking to be. If we get dressed up as Rav Kook or the Piaseczna Rebbe, of course we know we are not them, but this is what we are striving for.

My berachah, when we are going into *Parashat Tetzaveh* in preparation for Purim, is that we learn to rethink what clothing is. We dress, not to impress, but to direct ourselves. I am not putting on my clothing to impress someone else; rather, I am internalizing within myself who I want to be and what I want to become.

Parashat Ki Tisa

IN MEMORY OF ETHAN LAX, MY REBBI

LEARNING CONVERSATION

A week ago, I lost my closest friend. I wanted to start each *shiur* from now on with a character trait that I learned from Ethan Lax: Eitan Eliezer ben Mordechai *alav ha'shalom*. The character trait I wanted to add into this week is love of children. My wife, Tanya, and I spent a lot of time in Toronto, and Ethan spent a lot of time playing with my children and engaging them in some of the deepest conversations. Why did Ethan love children so much? Children are filled with dreams and ideas. A child is full of dreams. Ethan lived that life and he connected to children through that.

When we enter into *Ki Tisa*, we enter into the darkest moment in Jewish history. There is no way to fathom the failure we experienced. We were at the top of the mountain, and in such a short amount of time we fell so low. There are many different ideas regarding what caused this awful collapse, but I want to try and understand the story immediately before and after the *chet ha'egel*. The story right before the *chet ha'egel* is the story of Shabbat. Immediately after the *chet ha'egel*, we also hear about Shabbat. The question is, why does Shabbat surround the story of the *chet ha'egel*? How does that affect our understanding of the story of the *chet ha'egel*?

The *Sefat Emet* asks: What's the idea of Shabbat? The idea of Shabbat is recognizing the level that you can reach. What he means is that during the week, we're very immersed in things that we need to do. We need to work and do certain things that we can't do on Shabbat. Our lives become centered around necessity. But on Shabbat, everything you need to do, you can't do. You can't cook; you can't turn on lights; you

130

can't change things on Shabbat. What's left to do on Shabbat? Things that you want to do. The idea of Shabbat is to eliminate the work that you need to do and enable you to reflect and internalize life.

The *Sefat Emet* says that Shabbat makes us realize where we can reach. I think that if we ask why Shabbat surrounds the story of the golden calf, the answer is very simple. The question is not what we did, but what caused us to get there. How could a nation reach a level where they abandoned such greatness? I think the answer is that we forgot Shabbat. We were so involved in the idea of *na'aseh*, that we'll do *all* the mitzvot! But we forgot to remember where we wanted to get to. We forgot that the goal of Torah is not doing mitzvot, but we do them in order to change ourselves, our nation, and the world. That is what we're reminded of on Shabbat.

That Shabbat surrounds the *chet ha'egel* teaches us that failure usually doesn't stem from failure, but from forgetting where you want to go.

As I finish this idea, I want to connect it back to Ethan. I'm left with a void now that Ethan is gone. My world is shattered and broken. There was something different about his presence. What Ethan always expressed, especially to me, were his feelings about Shabbat. They always reminded me where to go, allowing me to orient my actions during the week to a greater purpose.

My berachah entering into this Shabbat after such a shattered week, is that we should understand and be capable of getting to that state where we can recognize our ability to remember, live, and understand Ethan's world. What he represented and lived for will prevent us from getting lost in the world of the things we need to do.

Parashat Ki Tisa

MEMORY FOR ETHAN: WANT BEFORE NEED

A WEEK AGO I got the news that one of my closest friends and someone with whom I really experienced a lot of life, Ethan Lax, passed away. I just want to start the *shiur* with a character trait that can be learned from Ethan.

One of the things that stood out for me was his respect for his parents. A couple of weeks ago, we got to Aroma, which was our coffee and learning place, and when we finished he told me that he was really worried about his parents because Jonathan had passed away recently, and it had been really difficult for them. So, he went to the cashier and bought an entire lunch for his parents. I think the idea of respecting one's parents really stood out for me with Ethan.

When we enter *Parashat Ki Tisa*, we enter into the darkest moment of Jewish history. Am Yisrael was on the highest level. We spoke to Hashem, and we received the Torah. And then immediately afterward, we shattered to the lowest level.

We abandoned our relationship. It is just a terrible experience in Am Yisrael's history. I often think the biggest question we have to ask is: How could it be that people fell so low? I think that if we look at the structure of the Torah it will give us a little bit of an insight of how to deal with this question of how can such great moments become so low so fast.

Immediately before the *chet ha'egel*, we hear about Shabbat, and right after the *chet ha'egel* we hear about Shabbat again. The story of the *chet ha'egel* is enwrapped in the concept of Shabbat. It is obvious that this structure is teaching us that we have to understand Shabbat in order to understand the *chet ha'egel*. What is it about Shabbat that if we would have remembered Shabbat, it would have prevented the failure of the *chet ha'egel*?

The *Sefat Emet* says that the concept of Shabbat involves recognizing that there is a difference between the week and Shabbat. During the week, we do everything that we need to do. We need to cook, so we cook. We need to eat, so we eat. We need to make fire, so we make fire. This is a life of needs. Shabbat comes in and eliminates all needs and it tells us: You are not allowed to do any more necessities. You are not allowed to cook or turn on light, and you cannot change anything because however it is, is the way that it is. When you don't have to change things or need to do anything, you suddenly recognize you have the ability to ask yourself a new question. It's not, "What do you need to do?" but "What do you want to do?" Shabbat comes to say to you, "Okay fine, you live a life of necessities like going to work and shul, putting on tzitzit, and lighting Shabbat candles. You are doing all the necessities, but can you transition from a world of need into a world of want?" When we forget what we want, we end up sitting by the *egel*. The *chet ha'egel* was the result of Am Yisrael forgetting what they wanted to reach. They knew they needed something, but they forgot what they wanted.

The fact that Shabbat surrounds the story of the *chet ha'egel* is saying that if you remember what you want, then when you need to do something, it's no longer demanding of you—it's enabling you. The obligations that you have enable you.

If I remember that I want to be with my family, then of course that comes with obligation, but that obligation becomes a privilege. If I remember that I feel that I care about the story of Am Yisrael, then that demand becomes a privilege because I know what I want. I want Am Yisrael to grow, and I want their joy, and I want them to grow. Therefore, my obligation is not going to cause me to do the sin of the *egel* because we will all make a *chet ha'egel*, meaning that the sin of the *egel* was a result of things becoming routine. We will all fail because if we make our relationship with Hashem into a relationship of need, then we are going to end up making an *egel*.

My berachah upon entering into Shabbat, as I trying to utilize, remember, and live the memory of Ethan, is very obvious to me. One of the things that stood out was his ability to create joy, to create dancing, to create honesty, and to be genuine. Ethan was very clear that he was not willing to make Judaism into just a need, but rather it stemmed from a want, from a dream, from a vision so that whatever he needed to do, he loved to do.

Parashat Ki Tisa

BROKEN WORLD, BUILDING PEOPLE

PARASHAT KI TISA: It's post-Purim, pre-Pesach, and we're in the midst of the coronavirus pandemic. We are adding in a little bit of meditation music in the background to be able to relax a little, to get our minds off the stress and questions we are all dealing with. We reach a famous moment in history in this parashah. Moshe Rabbeinu sees the *chet ha'egel*, the Sin of the Golden Calf, and he breaks the *Luchot*, tablets. There could have been many reactions; he could have screamed, or he could have done nothing. Yet he decided to break the *Luchot*. The Gemara brings different opinions on Moshe's action.[1] One of the opinions is that Hashem said to him "יישר כחך ששברת"—I praise you for breaking the *Luchot*." So, if Hashem is praising Moshe for breaking the *Luchot*, then we need to ask and analyze if there was something else Moshe was thinking when he was breaking the *Luchot*? If it was just a natural reaction of anger, then why did Hashem praise him? Maybe Moshe was giving a lesson that there is no such thing as endings. Even the broken *Luchot* have a purpose—even *Luchot* that you cannot read the letters on. The broken *Luchot* are inside the *Aron*. Moshe was saying that things that are shattered, are not what they look like; they demand creativity, activity, and they give you an opportunity to renew yourself.

So many levels of where we are right now, with school systems closing, people being locked in their homes, everyone being nervous about each other, and people not knowing if they have a job, imply that we are in a state of brokenness. The *Luchot* that we previously held onto have

---

1 *Shabbat* 87a.

been thrown onto the floor and broken. But Moshe was asking us if we know to take the broken *Luchot* and put them inside our homes. Do you realize that the broken *Luchot* are giving you an opportunity to put them into the *Aron*? They are telling you to hold onto things we were maybe not able to do before. Maybe we were not able to bring the broken *Luchot* into our homes; we forgot our homes. Maybe the Seder was just a conceptual thing, but now it is a practical thing. Just like in Mitzrayim when we were locked in, now too we are locked into our homes and our worlds. In this parashah Moshe was asking us whether we can look at the *shever*, brokenness. Are you able to take the broken *Luchot*, glue the pieces together, and be creative with them?

My berachah going into *Parashat Ki Tisa* is that although there are so many broken things—broken expectations, broken systems, and so many questions—we should have the privilege and the opportunity to try and be creative. Regular *chessed* might not work right now; we cannot just walk into a random place and give out chocolates. However, we need to think of creative *chessed* projects—sending out messages, thinking of empty homes people could use for their quarantines, making games on YouTube that people could use with their families, making *mishlo'ach manot* that help people use the time they have. *B'ezrat Hashem* we should all be *zocheh*, like Adi and I were today, when we had the *zechut* to go out into the living room and do math together for a long time. We need to be creative with the *shever*. May we give each other strength in new and creative ways, and may we be *zocheh* to only see Am Yisrael and the world find new ways of enjoying the world that we have been given.

Parashat Ki Tisa

BE AWARE

WHEN WE ENTER into *Parashat Ki Tisa*, we deal with the question of failure. It seems that there is no greater failure in history than to be standing at the foot of success, relationship, and anticipation that has been culminated and revived, and then to suddenly see it all shatter and crash. The difference between the moment when Hashem revealed Himself to the world, and the moment when this experience shattered. But what causes failure? And how do we have such high expectations and then end up in places that are the exact opposite?

Baruch Hashem, our Ohr Eytan's bar mitzvah is in one week. It's not easy to say that sentence. It's very, very, crazy to think about a child that in your eyes is still a baby, and he's now going up to the Torah and wearing tefillin. But we had an experience about a week ago. He had just started putting on tefillin, and then there was a day where he forgot to do so. He remembered when it was four p.m., and we were driving in the car, so we figured we had about an hour left and that when we got home, he'd put on tefillin. On the way back, Ohr Eytan asked me, "*Abba*, why is it so different to miss putting on tefillin as opposed to missing davening?" I said to him, "Ohr Eytan, you know, the difference with tefillin is that it is above us and every other mitzvah belongs to us." When we light Shabbat candles it's with our family, when we put on tzitzit it's ours, when we do *chessed* it's for other people, but it's really stemming from us. The idea of tefillin is that it's all about getting to the *tefillin shel rosh* which goes above the head. Given this, "The moment you have that responsibility, and you miss it, then the rest of Am Yisrael is missing something. The experience of tefillin feels much more severe because it's the concept that the actions you do as an individual are not

137

yours anymore, but they are much greater than you." Suddenly, we hit traffic and Ohr Eytan started getting nervous because he really didn't want to miss a day of tefillin. Miraculously, we remembered that my tefillin was in the car so we stopped on the side of the road and he put on tefillin. He came back in with the biggest smile and said to me, "I really reconnected with Am Yisrael!"

With the *chet ha'egel* there was one big mistake which was that Am Yisrael said, "עשה לנו אלהים—Make us gods."[1] They thought that they needed something for themselves. It's true that all of us have needs, but the idea of personal needs is irrelevant in comparison with our relationship with Torah. The idea of Torah learning is that obviously it can affect you, enable you, make you more responsible, make you happy, and bring you joy, but none of those are the foundation of the Torah. The idea of the Torah, when it's given, is that it's given to the entire nation. Not to say that it's to all of you, but it's conditional. It only works if you see your learning as part of a circle, a nation, a unity, a responsibility, and of a relationship that's much bigger and greater than yourself.

The idea of the *luchot* is that they are given through a foundational experience which recognized that the greatest privilege in the world is to understand and be aware of what the true self is. The true self is the realization and the understanding that the greatest present in the world that we received is the ability to know that our actions have an impact and connection to everyone in the past, future, and present. It has a connection to everything that's happened in the story of Am Yisrael. When the Torah is given to us, it's only on condition that we recognize this idea.

As we go into Pesach and we think about what we're celebrating, we should momentarily consider the matzah. We can see that it is very similar to chametz. They have the same ingredients, and the letters to spell each are identical—except for the *hei* and *chet* which is the difference of a little line, meaning that only a second differentiates them.

---

1   *Shemot* 32:1.

If we look at chametz, we see that it is very much focused on its own growth, and therefore, it causes destruction, while the matzah doesn't let itself grow—it never rises—and therefore leaves room for everyone else. That is real redemption. This is the story that we're trying to build ourselves up to as we get ready for Pesach.

I think that this is also the berachah that I'm trying to impart to Ohr Eytan, Tanya, Adiel, and Roni. It's the greatest *simchah* in the world to realize that the biggest present we could give ourselves is not to be accomplished, but to be aware. The more accomplished we are, the more we disconnect ourselves from others. The less we are involved with ourselves and the more aware we are of the opportunities, responsibilities, and privileges that we have, the more the Torah becomes something real.

My berachah, as we walk into *Parashat Ki Tisa* and *Parashat Parah*—which is the parashah that really deals with purifying ourselves from not being too engaged in ourselves—and as we only have three more weeks until Pesach, and as our family approaches the bar mitzvah of Ohr Eytan, is that we are all should be able to realize that truly being aware is so much deeper than being accomplished.

Parashat Pekudei

BIGGER THAN KNOWLEDGE

LEARNING CONVERSATION

A character trait from Ethan: A lot of us really enjoy food. One of the things that not many of us are great at is being healthy and knowing what foods are healthy and unhealthy. Ethan always taught me how to choose healthy food. It meant recognizing food as a gift, and not just something that's sustaining you.

There is a *pasuk* in *Parashat Pekudei* which is one of the most difficult in the entire Torah. The last five parshiyot have been preparations for Hashem to appear in the *Mishkan*. The Jews donated everything they had to build this *Mishkan*. But the closing *pasuk* of *Sefer Shemot* is "ולא יכול משה לבא אל אוהל מועד—Moshe could not enter the Tent of Meeting."[1] They prepared everything, but the result didn't happen. Moshe couldn't go in.

To try to understand what the idea behind this *pasuk* is, we can look in *Megillat Esther*. When we look into the Megillah, one of the most powerful sentences is "רוח והצלה יעמוד ליהודים ממקום אחר—Relief and deliverance will come to the Jews from someone else."[2] Mordechai tells Esther that she has the opportunity and privilege to help the Jewish people, but he wants her to understand that there's something bigger than her. If she doesn't participate, redemption would still happen.

The teachings of the Kabbalah explain that this sentence reveals two ways to look at the world. One way is that everything works on a system

---

1   *Shemot* 40:35.
2   *Esther* 4:14.

of reward and punishment based on your own actions. This is a system of logic.

But Mordechai tells Esther that not everything is dependent on logic and action. You can assist redemption, but redemption won't happen because you decided to step up. When we look at the end of *Sefer Shemot*, that is one of the messages Hashem was teaching us. On one hand, we do what we're supposed to do, and things work the way they're supposed to work. Things are logical, and they make sense. But some things are beyond our knowledge.

In *Masechta Sanhedrin*, it says that the era of Mashiach will come in its time but in another way. What does that mean? There are two ways Mashiach can come. Either we can bring him, or he'll come on his own. But you don't cause Mashiach to come. You don't define redemption. In the world, there is logic and there is emotion. There are things that make sense, and there's Hashem. The things that Hashem can do supersede logic.

When you look at Mordechai, who comes from Shevet Binyamin, he was very logical. Why? Binyamin was Yosef's brother, whose life was defined by logic. When Yosef did something wrong, he was thrown into a pit. When he did something right, he became a redeemer. Mordechai understands that, and he is defined by his actions.

Yes, there's logic, but you can't define life with logic. Use your logic, understand logic, try to bring redemption, but understand that there's another level. The other level is what we see when Moshe can't enter the *Mishkan*. It doesn't make sense. They did everything right, but still he couldn't go in. Hashem was teaching Am Yisrael that if you want to be happy, don't limit yourselves to logic and your own human understanding.

Parashat Vayakhel-Pekudei

A SHABBAT WORLD

WE ARE ENTERING into Shabbat after a full week of Shabbat. We had a full week of being home, and now it seems like Shabbat is going to be what we had all week. Specifically, we enter into *Parashat Vayakhel-Pekudei*, which describes the building of the *Mishkan*.

A lot of the commentaries try to understand why these parshiyot, whose focus is the *Mishkan*, begin with reference to Shabbat. There are a lot of halachot that we learn from this connection, and overall, there is a very strong link between the *Mishkan*, the Beit Hamikdash, and Shabbat. The question is: What is this link between Shabbat, the *Mishkan*, and the Mikdash?

There is a *melachah* that appears in *hilchot Shabbat* called the *melachah* of *hatmanah*, insulating. The *melachah* of *hatmanah* means that when you want to heat Shabbat food for the meal, you want to preserve the heat, but you cannot put it into something that adds heat. We see that there is a distinction in this idea of Shabbat that we want the food to be hot, but we need to preserve it and not add to it. The idea of Shabbat, through *hatmanah*, is that the goal of Shabbat is to preserve, continue. Whenever we are adding something, we lose the relationship with what we have.

There is a mitzvah called "עוסק במצוה פטור מן המצוה—One who is engaged in a mitzvah is exempt from a mitzvah" at that time. The *Ohr Zarua* asks, if someone is doing a mitzvah, are they required to do another? It says that you must understand the goal of a mitzvah is to be connected. If you are trying to do another mitzvah, this must mean that you do not really understand the goal of the mitzvah. By doing another mitzvah you are contradicting the essence of the mitzvah. By looking for another, you become disconnected. The same holds true with Shabbat. Whenever you add heat to something, you change its essence, and you are not connected. The idea of Shabbat is to preserve, to hold, to be aware, to be understanding, and to be connected to what is in front of you.

How does this connect to the Mikdash? We know that a lot of messages have been coming out lately that Mashiach is coming, that the world is being perfected, and that this Shabbat will be the first one that the entire world will be keeping. But the idea of the Mikdash is that you have a place in the world that has everything. It deals with physicality; the Mikdash deals with gold, copper, animals, sins, the *Kodesh Hakodashim*, the Holy of Holies, bread, and fires. The goal of the Mikdash is that it has everything, and so you do not need to go anywhere else. So really, Shabbat is the definition of the Beit Hamikdash—that you are able to be in a world where you realize that what is in front of you is everything you need.

Admittedly this is very difficult. When we were all living in a world where we had so many other things like shopping centers, stores, restaurants, and planes—we lived in a world of so much addition—we felt contracted, disabled, and scared. But maybe the idea of the end of *Sefer Shemot* is that the need to always search for more is exactly the opposite of Shabbat and the Beit Hamikdash. We need to look for more, not because there are more objects, but because what is in front of us has so much more to it. We have been with our families for a week now, but there's so much more that we could learn about our spouses, children, and ourselves.

My berachah as we enter into the end of *Sefer Shemot*, into a world that is so different, is that we should be able to really internalize how different Shabbat is.

PURE SILENCE

The bar mitzvah of Ohr Eytan (Rav Yair's oldest son)

WE KNOW THAT *Vayakhel-Pekudei* deals with the actual building of the *Mishkan*. According to the *Ramban*, the *Mishkan* was a *tikkun* for *maamad Har Sinai*, where essentially things failed but it was all rectified through the *Mishkan*. So how does the *Mishkan* fix the brokenness of *maamad Har Sinai*? Yet beyond this, it is noteworthy that in the *haftarah*, the main word emphasized there is *"bayit."* But why is that so essential to us? I think that both these questions can connect together to form one idea.

When we backtrack to the *chet ha'egel*, there is a beautiful *Rashi* there which describes the second time Moshe ascended on Har Sinai to receive the *Luchot*. The *pasuk* says, "ואיש לא יעלה עמך—No one else shall come up with you."[1] *Rashi* says on this, "הראשונות ע״י שהיו בתשואות וקולות וקהלות, שלטה בהן עין רעה—אין לך יפה מן הצניעות—Because the first tablets were given amidst great noises and alarms and a vast assembly, the 'evil eye' had power over them [they did not endure]—there is no finer quality than to be alone with Hashem!"[2]

If we look at the *chet ha'egel* we learn that what caused this destruction, according to *Rashi*, is that *Matan Torah* was so revealed. It was so loud. It was so big. We sometimes think that the loudly singing and shouting out, "הקדוש ברוך הוא אנחנו אוהבים אותך—Hashem, we love you!" is a virtue. However, *Moreinu v'Rabbeinu*, Rav Re'em, says that is exactly

---

1   *Shemot* 34:3.
2   Ibid.

the problem. He says that true love and real love is not measured by how much noise we make, and it's not measured in quantity. It's what we think, but that's exactly the problem. The bigger it is, the more irrelevant it is. The louder it is, the more short-term it is. Therefore, when Moshe Rabbeinu went up to Har Sinai, he went alone. It was a very quiet, personal experience for him and Hashem.

The *Mishkan* had specifications, and it was detailed oriented. You went from A to B to C. Some people went here, and some people went there, and when you went into the *Kodesh Hakodashim*, it was so small and so quiet. That is the *tikkun* of *maamad Har Sinai*. It teaches us that if we really want things to last, if we want things to be built, if we want things to continue, and if we want things to be relevant, we have to translate them into details. We have to reveal them quietly and with harmony and not think that louder is better. Quite the opposite! The more hidden and the quieter it is, the stronger it will be.

For Ohr Eytan, I think that I, Tanya, Adiel, and Roni could obviously testify that quiet waters go deeper and deeper. It is something that is very evident with Ohr Eytan that he has so much to say, but he doesn't say it out loud; he doesn't scream it. Instead, he whispers it. That whisper is like the *Kodesh Hakodashim*. That whisper is like the *tikkun* of how we used to think the louder it is, the better it is. Ohr Eytan is an expression of the idea that more real it is, the more you can see it in someone's face, and they don't even have to say it.

As we go into *Parashat HaChodesh*, the same concept applies to our redemption. When we left Egypt, you would think they would have gone out into the streets to celebrate the redemption by yelling on the top of their lungs. We all know the scene from *Shawshank Redemption* when Andy Dufresne leaves prison after nineteen years, and he picks up his hands and yells at the top of his lungs. We would also think that after 210 years of slavery in Egypt the Jewish people would yell, scream, celebrate, and make barbeques. Instead, Hashem said, "Lock yourselves in your homes." Realize that what's going to make it last is not revealing everything in the public domain, but rather, making your home so full with the redemption that it doesn't even need to be announced. Real redemption is celebrated at the core of our family. It is celebrated locked up in our homes because that's the message of *yetziat Mitzrayim*. Mitzrayim revealed everything and it went really high, but it exploded and didn't last. The moment of *yetziyat Mitzrayim* was so large we couldn't grasp or maintain all of it. We lock ourselves in a little house, and in that home, we celebrate our redemption. We are announcing to the world that the only way for the future to be better is if we come back to the mundane of life, into the reality of life, and into the quiet areas of life. Those are the eternal relationships that we are searching for.

We are all so excited for his bar mitzvah. We know his *abba* is sometimes very loud and sometimes he'll scream or yell. The friendship that, *baruch Hashem*, I have built with Ohr Eytani is expressed on the walks that we take together on a Shabbat night, when Ohr Eytani will teach me the beauty of the harmony of waters that are just so pure that they don't need to make so much sound. Our berachah going into this Shabbat is that Ohr Eytani should be able to lead Am Yisrael. It should help him enjoy Am Yisrael, and it should help him recognize that he can do things in such a way that the *Kodesh Hakodashim* did for all of Am Yisrael.

Parashat Vayikra

I, WITH US

OPENING QUESTIONS

1. How is *Sefer Vayikra* different than the other *sefarim* in Chumash?
2. What do you think is the main message of the world of *korbanot*?
3. Why is the opening phrase for the world of *korbanot* "*Adam ki yakriv mikem*"?
4. What is the right balance between a person's individual uniqueness and their communal obligations?

LIVING THE LEARNING

Sefer Vayikra is different. The *sefarim* until *Vayikra* are interesting and story-oriented. They have a lot of different issues going on, and every parashah has a different concept behind it. You walk into *Sefer Bamidbar* and *Sefer Devarim*, and it is very clear that we are preparing to enter into the land. *Vayikra* is like the "middle child" in a way; it is so unclear and seems boring. It is constantly dealing with the world of *korbanot* and *tum'ah* and *taharah*. The question is, what purpose does *Sefer Vayikra* play?

The Midrash teaches that when we start teaching a child Torah, we should begin from *Sefer Vayikra*. This opens up a demand to search for a deeper perspective on the world of *Vayikra* and the concept of *korbanot* that would make it the "go to" *sefer* for children. So, in an amazing way, the *Sefat Emet* looks at the opening sentence of *Sefer Vayikra* and

147

addresses maybe one of the greatest questions that the book is dealing with. The *pasuk* he focuses on says, "אדם כי יקריב מכם—When any of you presents an offering of cattle from all of you."[1] The introduction to the world of *korbanot*, sacrifices, has four words. If we look at these four words, the first and last words are opposites. The first, *adam*, is that it's an individual experience. The fourth word says *mikem* and it is sort of unnecessary. What is the idea of bringing in the communal experience of *mikem*, them?

In the times that we live in, there has been a transition from the journey of commitment to the journey of connection.

We can see this paradigm shift between the builders of Israel in the beginning and the society and mindset of today. *Baruch Hashem*, I just took a whole group of kids to Israel for the Shalva marathon, and we had the opportunity to look at what life was like in Kfar Etzion in 1948. There was a lot of commitment. They were people who didn't really want you to know their names, but just wanted you to know their message. The only thing that mattered was the commitment to a message. When you look at us today, there is a very strong emphasis on connection: our connection to mitzvot, our connection to *tefillah*, our connection to our families, and our connection to our jobs. We therefore see a transition from the conversation of commitment to the conversation of connection. I think that in *Sefer Vayikra* we can see a way that deals with these two things in an incredible way.

The *Sefat Emet* says on the word *adam*, "ליתן מפנימיות כחו—A person must sacrifice from his inner strength."[2] To understand this, we have to realize that we are all different. We are not the same people. It's true we might all have eyes, ears, and noses but we are not the same. Externally, there might be similarities, but internally we are different worlds. *Sefer Vayikra* is the transition from the leadership of an individual to an opportunity for the entire nation. That is the transition of *Sefer Vayikra*. If you look in *Sefer Bereishit* there are four central figures: Avraham, Yitzchak, Yaakov, and Yosef. If you look at *Sefer Shemot* there is one

---

1   *Vayikra* 1:2.
2   *Sefat Emet, Vayikra* 1.

name: Moshe. *Sefer Vayikra* comes along and says that the message for Am Yisrael was that there had been a need, but it wasn't the goal. The concept of *korbanot* is to find space for different people and to create space for everyone. It's not healthy to have leadership without a nation. We develop the leadership aspect, yet where is the nation? The idea of an *adam*, man, is that he has the ability to realize that the world of *korbanot* means that it's not just Moshe Rabbeinu's story, it is not just Rav Kook's story, and it is not just the Lubavitcher Rebbe's story, either. The question then becomes, what is *mikem*, them? The *Sefat Emet* says that you have to realize, "שהגם שכל אחד יתן ענין שלי יהי' ע"י הכנסת עצמו בתוך כלל ישראל—even when everyone is expressing their individuality, it must be done within the nation." The means to become aware of our uniqueness, we must relate it to the nation. He is saying that yes, you are an individual, but what will enable your specialty to last? What will make it real and not selfish and self-serving? Only if it is within *mikem*, them. If your expression isn't within the context of a bigger story, then it will be strong and then suddenly evaporate. The eternal ability of an individual is that they are aware of the fact that their story is connected to *our* story.

The last journey that I made to Israel was for a week at the end of my *shlichut* in Toronto. I went with a group of fifty-six kids and for the first four days I wanted them to feel *our* story. You are walking around and everywhere you go, you are part of a story that is big. On the last day, I tried to get each of the kids to understand that once there is a bigger story, and you relate your personal page or chapter to the book, then your chapter will last forever.

My berachah as we are entering into the month of Nissan and into the journey of redemption, is for Am Yisrael to realize that we have a message. The message is that individuality within commitment and connection with a feeling of being part of something greater will last forever. However, a connection that is disabling commitment, where the emphasis of an individual is without the feeling of a unit—like teaching someone to become a great, learned Torah scholar without the feeling of "I am part and so significant to Am Yisrael"—ultimately becomes destruction. Your personal growth becomes selfish. The most important message for us is that when we are teaching people to develop and learn to connect, it cannot be in contrast to commitment. *B'ezrat Hashem*, this Shabbat I am giving us all a berachah that we should realize that the greatest individuality and growth comes from the feeling that your story will affect our story.

LIVING THE LEARNING

Choose a historical figure from Medinat Yisrael's story (Menachem Begin, Rabin), and read the autobiography of this person to get the feeling of what it means to look at an individual who truly feels a part of the big story of Am Yisrael.

Parashat Vayikra

THE BEAUTY OF PHYSICAL

LEARNING CONVERSATION

A character trait from Ethan: A lot of us speak about working out and think about working out, but we don't actually work out. Ethan and I would often talk about that, including during one of our *chavrutas*. He told me that if you want to work on your spiritual side, you have to first work on your physical side. He showed me that the ability to work on your physical body affects your ability to grow spiritually.

When we enter into *Sefer Vayikra* and approach the holiday of Purim, we need to address a question. Sefer *Vayikra* is a world of *korbanot*, sacrifices, and animals. We learn which animals are kosher and which animals to sacrifice.

There's something interesting about the Beit Hamikdash. What would you expect to see at the entrance of the Beit Hamikdash, Hashem's house? Maybe *sefarim* or people dancing and singing, or other spiritually inspiring things? But that was not the case. The entrance into the Beit Hamikdash was full of animals—not very inviting. In fact, it's very physical! Why was the entrance into the home of Hashem filled with physical beings as opposed to things that might inspire us spiritually?

We need to think about Purim to answer this question. When we enter into Purim, the holiday is infused with physicality, in contrast to Chanukah, which focuses on spirituality. Purim goes to the opposite extreme and focuses on food, costumes, and the Megillah which speaks about the Jews indulging themselves at the king's party. Why do we celebrate with so much physicality? Isn't that a problem?

Purim teaches us a lesson. The essence of a person's growth is not measured by how high he can go, but rather whether he can grasp lofty

151

ideas and apply them to everyday life. Purim teaches us that the highest level we can reach is when we can deal with physical challenges. We shouldn't run away from physicality, but learn from it and incorporate it into our lives.

Physicality is an opportunity, not a problem. It's full of passion and desire. Where there is desire, there is change and excitement. The idea of Purim gives us a different perspective than *Sefer Vayikra*. The entrance into the house of Hashem doesn't remove us from physicality because it challenges us to incorporate it into our lives.

My berachah as we enter *Sefer Vayikra* and approach Purim is that we should realize that Hashem built a physical world and gave us physical desires. We need to understand that physicality has the ability to take us to higher levels of spirituality. The physicality should enable us to recognize our true spirituality.

YOU ARE THE GARBAGE YOU PICK UP

Shabbat HaGadol

> "If you aren't taking out the garbage, you are garbage."

OPENING QUESTIONS

1. Who do you think is the ideal person to take out the garbage in the Beit Hamikdash?
2. What do you think of Pesach cleaning?

LEARNING CONVERSATION

We all experienced Rosh Chodesh Nissan which means that we all started cleaning up our homes. We start going into the little nooks, corners, and cabinets, and start taking out all the garbage that we pushed to the side the whole year. There is an important question for all of us to ask. How is this preparing us for Pesach? How does all of this cleaning, gathering of garbage, and all these different things connect us to Pesach?

Through the parashah I want to be able to rethink the experience of cleaning our homes. There is a very unique mitzvah that we deal with at the beginning of our parashah, *Parashat Tzav*: the mitzvah of *haramat ha'deshen*, removing the ashes. *Baruch Hashem*, in the Beit Hamikdash there was a lot of activity—a lot of *korbanot*, a lot of people, a lot of music, and also there was a lot of garbage. That's just the way it is. When there is more life, there is more garbage. When there is more activity, there is more garbage. The more the place is alive, the more garbage you will see.

153

Therefore, in the Beit Hamikdash there was a lot of garbage—it was a place that is full of life. In the beginning everyone would say that the garbage was a problem, so they needed to get rid of the garbage. Since the problem was the garbage, they thought to just get it out of the way. You would think they would just invite a random guy from the street and tell him to pick up the garbage and take it out of there, whatever it is. The Torah teaches us something that transforms the Kohanim, the Beit Hamikdash, and maybe even on a certain level the core of Judaism. The mitzvah comes and teaches us that the garbage can only be lifted by a Kohen who was wearing *bigdei kehunah*. Although you would have thought garbage is just something we move out of the way, it's not. We need a unique person, a leader of our nation, to wear his most special clothing to pick up the garbage. The obvious question is: How does it make sense to take the leader of the Jewish people, wearing his most expensive clothing, and ask him to pick up the garbage?

We know that in the world that we live in—and I've been *zocheh* to be in many high schools this year—the people picking up the garbage are not the principals. We hire someone external who doesn't have anything else to do with the school, and it's their job to pick up the garbage. Says Beit Hamikdash: No. It cannot be that as a Rosh Yeshiva, principal, teacher, parent, or whoever you are, that you view garbage as a problem, because garbage is a lesson. What is the lesson? Says the *Sefat Emet*, "כי כפי מה שנשרף הפסולת. כמו כן מתגלה הקדושה באדם".[1] A personality is defined by the way that they interact with garbage. This means that you might see the things that no one cares about. No one is excited about garbage, and no one gets all inspired about someone picking up garbage. People get inspired by fireworks, or a talented chazzan, or an amazing businessman. All of that is inspiring, but garbage is certainly not inspiring. Says the Torah, you have to redefine leadership and redefine garbage. The symbol of garbage is that no one else cares about it. The question is, Are you willing to be real enough to pick up garbage?

---

1   *Sefat Emet, Tzav* 4.

I know that for me, when I was growing up in Yeshivat Otniel, there were many different *shuirim* that I went to. I think the deepest and best lesson that I ever learned was watching my Rosh Yeshiva, Rav Re'em. Every single day at 1:40 p.m. at the end of lunch, Rav Re'em would walk over to the garbage with three garbage bags, and without anyone watching, he would clean up the garbage. You think to yourself, this is Rav Re'em! This is the guy who knows all the Torah, and this is the guy who has fire coming out of his eyes. You are looking at him picking up garbage, and that means that he's real. He is not just image or what looks good—he is real. Garbage is part of life, and I want to be part of life, and therefore by picking up garbage, it redefines leadership. Leadership is not about people who lead others, but people who lead themselves. I think if we return to our first question about cleaning for Pesach, we see that on Pesach we deal with exalted ideas. We could sit around and speak about what slavery is, and what redemption is, and what the secret of matzah is. I think that there is something so much deeper about Pesach. Pesach is asking us the first question which is the entrance code into Judaism: Are you real or are you all about image? This will be measured through the question of who and how one picks up the garbage of life.

My berachah as we enter into Shabbat HaGadol in preparation for the biggest night of the year, the night of the Seder, is that we sit around and think to ourselves in relation to this mitzvah of picking up garbage and ask the question: Are we real people or are we image people?

LIVING THE LEARNING

In light of cleaning for Pesach, at the end of each day of cleaning, look at all the garbage bags that were collected during that day of cleaning, and write an idea that you learned from this pile of garbage that you'll share at the Seder.

FOCUSING ON MATZAH

LEARNING CONVERSATION

What does matzah symbolize? We say in *Maggid* that there are three things we need to say on the Seder night, according to Rabban Gamliel: Pesach, Matzah, and Maror. We say that the reason we eat matzah is because when we left Egypt, we didn't have enough time for the dough to rise. Therefore, when we eat the matzah, we remember that we left Egypt with haste. However, most of us grow up thinking that we rushed out because we were scared of the Egyptians. But the Torah actually says the night we left was *Makkat Bechorot*. The Egyptians were mourning, not chasing us.

Thus, matzah also represents the exact moment we were redeemed from Egypt. So, what is the matzah teaching us regarding the difference between slavery and redemption?

The *Sefat Emet* explains that the reason the matzah had to be eaten hastily was because there are forty-nine "gates" of impurity, and B'nei Yisrael was at the lowest gate. Purity and impurity are complicated topics, as there are different levels. The reason something may be impure could be for many different reasons. At the moment of *yetziat Mitzrayim*, Am Yisrael was on the lowest level of *tum'ah*. They didn't believe in Moshe or Hashem. They looked, thought, and acted like the Egyptians. *Perek beit* of *Sefer Shemot* tells us that they would beat one another and that they hated each other! If B'nei Yisrael had sunk any deeper, they would have never come back.

If Am Yisrael would have stayed in Egypt, they would have reached level fifty of *tum'ah*, and they would have never been able to return. So, the reason they had to run was not because of the Egyptians but because of themselves. One more second in Egypt could have been the difference between freedom and eternal slavery.

The rush was to teach us that we could have never left Egypt if we stayed for one more second. Similarly, the only difference between matzah and bread is time. If you let dough rise for eighteen minutes, it's chametz. If it rises for seventeen minutes and fifty-nine seconds, it's not, even though the ingredients are exactly the same.

Additionally, the spelling of chametz and matzah both have a *mem* and a *tzaddi*. The only difference between the two words is a *hei* versus a *chet*. These two letters are exactly the same except for a small line on the *chet* that the *hei* doesn't have. The only difference between greatness and failure is the way you look at a moment and understand that it is infinitely significant. We live in a time where we value quantity over quality. But in only one tiny second, we could have become eternal slaves in Egypt. In that same second, we released ourselves from slavery.

When we eat matzah, we need to understand that the way we do something is significant. Is it a dinner with our family if we're all on our phones? Did we make a berachah if we didn't internalize what we're saying? The matzah teaches us that the true redemption is when we stop focusing on quantity. We need to stop thinking that numbers define us. Numbers are dangerous because they don't let us feel the symbolism and opportunity of the moment.

My berachah, as we enter into Pesach, is that we should understand that the reason the matzah couldn't rise was in order to teach us that we need to recognize the value of every second. Even our smallest actions will affect us if we are focused on them.

Parashat Shemini

NADAV AND AVIHU: THE SILENT BELIEVERS

PARASHAT SHEMINI goes into one of the most important moments in Am Yisrael's history. Even after we sinned during the *chet ha'egel*, Hashem still continued revealing Himself and being active in our lives. The sins do not define us, and the relationship is eternal. And then there was a very big moment during which the greatest tragedy occurred, the loss of Nadav and Avihu.

If we think about the context of this combination of these two things coming in at the same parashah, we'll see that it is also very much linked to the excitement of eleven days from now until Yom Ha'atzmaut. Even though we were abandoned and thrown out from the land, we still came back and received this second chance to see Hashem's presence in our lives.

When we are thinking about these two things, maybe we can learn something from Aharon HaKohen. We know that Aharon HaKohen's reaction to the loss of Nadav and Avihu was silence. A lot of us don't really understand the depth of silence. What does it mean that we don't understand the depth of silence? We live in a world of words, meaning the more you say, the more accomplished you are. That is the world in which we live in, a world of words. And what you don't say is obviously not real. Given this reality, maybe Aharon HaKohen taught us a new way of looking at life. He was saying that the words we say have nothing to do with who we are. The words we say have to do with Hashem's ability to give us the chance to affect, to help, to save, and to give to other people. Words are not the essence; words are your impact, and your essence is your silence. Silence is where you are able to be honest with yourself. No one knows, and no one cares, and in that silence you're able to understand who you are. It could be that maybe Aharon HaKohen wasn't silent only out of this feeling of pain, but maybe he was also giving over who Nadav and Avihu were.

When we look at the characters of Nadav and Avihu we never hear anything about them. We don't hear any words. The only thing we know about Nadav and Avihu is that they entered into the *Kodesh Hakodashim*. The *Kodesh Hakodashim* is very different from the *Chatzer*. The *Chatzer* (courtyard) was a place of words. It was a place of impact, and it was a place of effect. The *Kodesh Hakodashim* was a place where no one was with you and there really were no words, just silence. Maybe in Aharon's silence, he wasn't only experiencing his pain, but he was revealing who Nadav and Avihu were. They were walking *Kodshei Hakodashim*. Moshe and Aharon both had a huge impact on all of Klal Yisrael, but in order for Am Yisrael to rebuild their relationship with Hashem, it is important to first realize that our true identity is not what we do for others. It is a beautiful thing that we care about, that we impact, and that we give, but if there isn't a place of silence or *Kodesh Hakodashim*, then we could possibly end up using other people as a way of running away from being honest and facing the truth. Maybe Nadav and Avihu, through Aharon, are the people of silence. Maybe they don't have autobiographies or books about them, but what they do have is the identity of people that lived in a way that wasn't only about words. They were essentially about being real with what you believe. Even if you say something, it doesn't mean you are real. Even if you yell something, it doesn't mean you are real. The real identity comes through silence and identifying with what you believe in. Maybe the silence of Aharon is saying that there's something called *anshei milim*, people of words, and something called *anshei demamah*, people of silence. The *anshei demamah* are people who believe so much in what they believe in that they don't even need to say it. That is something very different from the world we live in, and it's not something we experience often.

To return to what we were saying earlier, Yom Ha'atzmaut might be a day that we have the opportunity to see the impact and a day where we see the effect in what we're doing for the world, but I think one of the things that we might need before all that is the silence of Yom HaShoah.

The silence of Yom HaShoah says two things: One is that it's the biggest tragedy and something that you cannot give answers to. It is simply just the greatest pain in the world. Period. Aharon might be teaching us, as well, that we might have not met these people, but they are the *Kodesh Hakodashim*. The *Kodesh Hakodashim* of Eretz Yisrael are those six million—the six million whose names we don't know. We don't have the books, and we might not have their autobiographies, but the level that they lived on, and the lifestyle that they created, is something that showed us what we have to sacrifice for Eretz Yisrael.

As we walk into this week of *Parashat Shemini* and we learn about Nadav and Avihu, we see that there's a parashah mixing the greatest tragedy in the world with the greatest new level of opportunity. I think we also have to learn from Aharon HaKohen that he's showing the world that we need to also learn how to be silent. We are so great and loving, we are so involved in giving and doing, but at the same time we don't have enough faith in what we believe in that we don't need to always share. We don't need to always impact, and we don't need to always change everyone around us in order for us to be real with ourselves. We can also just stand silently in *Shemoneh Esreh* and feel the silence. Maybe that is the condition for Eretz Yisrael. Maybe Eretz Yisrael is a place of tremendous noise, a building of a nation, and a building of a community, but you cannot do that if you don't have silence before. Avraham Avinu is the builder of Eretz Yisrael and it's an amazing thing that we meet him at the age of seventy-five going to the land. But before that there was tremendous silence. The Midrash tries to fill in who he was before, and they say maybe he was breaking the idols. But maybe Avraham Avinu, for the first seventy-five years of his life, was silent. Maybe he was just believing enough in what he was doing that he didn't need to show it to everyone, and as a result of that he was able to come to Eretz Yisrael.

We should be *zocheh* to reach that level of *demamah*, silence, and to reach that level that it is not only when others approve of what we say that it makes it real. The fact that we don't need to say it is proof that we believe in it enough that it's going to have an impact. *B'ezrat Hashem*, we should experience that *demamah* on both levels—obviously on the level that there are no answers for the tremendous tragedy of the loss of the Nadav and Avihus of the world—but at the same time, we also have to ask ourselves if we are also learning that they are the founders of Eretz Yisrael. They were people and had the lifestyles that we may have not heard about, but their existence is something that demands of us to continue that lifestyle. It demands of us to continue saying to ourselves that we must not only impact others but to also believe enough that we don't only need to impact others.

Parashat Tazria

PESACH: EARN TO YEARN

LEARNING CONVERSATION

The idea of the four children comes from the Torah. But when we're introduced to this concept, the focus is on the questions, not the children. The *pasuk* says, "וְהָיָה כִּי יִשְׁאָלְךָ בִנְךָ מָחָר לֵאמֹר מַה זֹּאת"—And when, in time to come, a child of yours asks you, saying, 'What does this mean?'"[1] The subject of the *pasuk* is the questions, not the children. Otherwise, it would have said something like "When your children will ask you…" not "When you will be asked by your children."

One of the biggest themes of the Seder is questions. But why ask questions, and why specifically now? We can ask questions at any time! Why are questions an essential part of the Seder? And what do questions mean?

There's a Gemara in *Masechta Pesachim* that says that if the son is smart, he asks the questions. However, if he's not smart, the wife asks the questions. Again, we see that the focus isn't on the child, but on the question. If the focus is on the children and the children aren't smart, then there will be no questions. The idea of the Four Questions is that even if the child isn't smart enough to ask the questions, the questions have to be asked anyway by the wife. But if the wife can't ask the question either, the Gemara says that the man should ask himself.

We think the reason we ask questions is to get an answer. But on the Seder night, if no one can ask the questions, you need to ask yourself! But what's the point? Shouldn't we ask someone else who knows more,

---

1   *Shemot* 13:14.

and probably knows the answer? But the idea of the question isn't the answer; it's the fact that you're asking. Even if there's no one to ask, you ask yourself. The Gemara is teaching us how to look at questions. The idea of the question is the question itself. We're not asking in order to get an answer; we're asking because the experience of asking changes you.

You can see the development of the child through the questions they ask through the years. They'll ask very internal questions, then more general questions, and then they'll say something personal about their questions. The questions you're asking show who you are and what you're thinking about.

Sometimes at the end of a question there's an exclamation mark. That's not a question; it's a statement in the context of a question. The person "asking" is not looking for an answer. Even if you answer them, their mindset doesn't allow them to internalize it. However, the people who genuinely ask a question are engaged and are truly searching for answers. If they're actually yearning, then try to answer their question.

The Gemara is teaching us that the focus should be on the questions. When, how, and to whom you ask the questions shows who you are. But why now? Why are we asking questions at the Seder? Questions are the foundation of Judaism. Judaism is based on questions because yearning is so much more important than you think.

Yesterday, I attended the funeral of Zechariah Baumel, z"l, whose body was missing for thirty-seven years after he was killed in Lebanon in 1982. I remember thinking about him as a child, but I had a feeling that eventually we would just forget about him and move on. But Zechariah's father never moved on. He yearned from the moment he lost him to get his body back. When I was at the funeral with thousands of people, there was a sense of yearning.

The idea of the Seder night is to ask us if we're yearning for something. At the end of the Seder there's a *minhag* to read *Shir Hashirim*. At the end of the book it says, "ברח דודי ודמה לך לצבי"—Run, my beloved, swift as a gazelle."[2] The end of the story is missing a relationship. The *dod*,

---

2   *Shir Hashirim* 8:14.

beloved, is running away! The end of *Shir Hashirim* is not only asking us if we got to the chuppah, but did we yearn for it? A lot of us want something, but when we don't get it, we stop wanting it. Don't!

It took thirty-seven years to bring a person back home, but we brought him back because we yearned. The questions are so essential on the night of the Seder because they are the foundation of Am Yisrael.

PESACH: IT TAKES TIME

THE SEFAT EMET says that the name of a holiday speaks to its essence. So, let's try and understand the name of the holiday, Pesach.

The simplest way of explaining the name of Pesach is that Hashem Himself passed over the homes of the Jewish people during *Makkat Bechorot*, and the Jewish firstborns were saved. But the question is: Why is that the essence of the holiday? There are a lot of other things we could have named the holiday after, but we focus on Hashem passing over the homes of Am Yisrael.

Many of our rituals are structured in a certain way. Many times, we prepare seven days for a revelation on the eighth day. One example is the seven days of *yemei milu'im*, the seven days that the Jewish people prepared the *Mishkan*. On the eighth day, they waited for Hashem to come down. Also, during *sefirat ha'omer*, we count seven weeks of seven days, then on the fiftieth day—which is equivalent to the eighth day—Hashem gave us the Torah. So too, we wait for a *brit milah* for seven days after the birth, and then we perform the mitzvah on the eighth day.

The concept of seven and then eight is that we're always recognizing that it's our job is to prepare, and then we can receive a revelation from Hashem. There's only one time where it's the opposite, where we first get a present and then prepare, and that's on Pesach. The *Korban Pesach* is on the fourteenth of Nissan, the day when we were redeemed. Then we have seven days of eating matzah and celebrating Pesach. At all other times, we need to earn the present. But on Pesach, we're given the present even though we didn't earn it.

The only way you can work on your relationship with Hashem is if you realize that it was all initiated by Hashem, and not by you. Today, there's so much focus on earning your reward in your relationship with Hashem, but you can only do that if you realize that first you were given an eternal, unconditional love that had nothing to do with who you are and what you do.

There's a *minhag* to read *Shir Hashirim* after completing the Haggadah. Why? To recognize Hashem's eternal love. We also don't say *k'riat Shema* before going to sleep on the Seder night because it's *leil shimurim*, a night where we're protected. The idea of Pesach is to realize that Hashem chose you before you chose him. He chose you, and nothing will ever break or destroy that.

So why Pesach? The idea of Pesach is that Hashem did something for us that we didn't earn. We were not ready for *yetziat Mitzrayim*. But that's why Pesach is so important. That's why we emphasize that Hashem himself, and not a messenger, took us out of Egypt. The idea of a relationship with Hashem is realizing that he believes in you even more than you believe in yourself.

My berachah as we enter the Seder is that we should recognize that the things we have been given by Hashem show us not what we earned but how much Hashem loves us. That is real redemption, that your ability is defined by the fact that something eternal chose you.

Parashat Tazria-Metzora

A PATIENT REDEMPTION

WE ARE IN THE MIDST of a very unique week where we have Rosh Chodesh on Monday and Tuesday, leading directly into Yom HaZikaron on Wednesday, and immediately into Yom Ha'atzmaut on Thursday. It is a week that we really want to try and understand in connection to the parashah. We want to discover the symbolism of Rosh Chodesh, the combination of Yom HaZikaron and Yom Ha'atzmaut, and why *Tazria-Metzora* this year is linked to this journey.

If we know about the concept of *tzaraat*, there's just a few things to focus on. The first is that when we're looking at *tzaraat*, it is a very long process. We first have to identify it, then if it's questionable, we wait for seven days, and we check again. Then if it continues, we then have to wait another seven days, and during this entire time the person is in total isolation.

We want to focus on these two things and connect them to this week. The first being the indirectness of *tzaraat*, with its variables and clarifications, and the second the duration of the process and why the isolation is for so long. I think these two things can very much help us understand the inner message of *tzaraat*.

Tzaraat is obviously a disease, and we know it comes from spiritual deficiencies such as *lashon hara* or jealousy. It then comes out on our skin, clothing, or homes. The difference between a physical problem and a spiritual problem is really measured by the amount of time. Physical problems are very often seen immediately and are treated immediately. If someone has a cut, you immediately see the blood and you immediately put a band-aid on it. The problem with spiritual problems is that they don't happen suddenly, and it takes a long time to see their results.

167

No one wakes up one morning and says, "I'm leaving Hashem!" Instead, it is a journey and a process where they begin from one challenge and another challenge and another challenge. Then, after a culmination of different difficulties, they end up, *chas v'shalom*, leaving Hashem. But it is never something that happens suddenly.

Significantly, the same is true when we try to cure ourselves from a spiritual problem. Everyone wants to change, because no one wants to be lazy, no one wants to be jealous, and no one wants to degrade other people. Even though we may want to be different, we have to realize that these changes don't happen immediately. There is a lot of time that we have to spend curing ourselves from the spiritual problems.

Tanya and I, *baruch Hashem*, just celebrated our fifteenth anniversary and we often say to each other that we've been fighting about the same things for fifteen years. It could also be that after seventy, eighty, or ninety years of marriage, we'll probably say the same thing. We are still fighting about the same things, because spiritual problems are always revealed either by the amount of time that they are caused, or by the amount of time that it takes to cure them. Therefore, *tzaraat* is something that requires a long process. I think if we connect this to the week that we're in, we'll see that it gives us a new mindset on Rosh Chodesh, Yom HaZikaron, and Yom Ha'atzmaut.

It is very weird that on Rosh Chodesh we say half-*Hallel* because no one was killed on this day and nothing bad happened. What is the reason that we could only say half-*Hallel*, as if it's not such a complete *simchah*?

The answer is that the idea of Rosh Chodesh is connecting to the moon, which is always going through a journey and a process. On Rosh Chodesh the moon is the smallest size that it can be, meaning that Rosh Chodesh is revealing to us this concept of patience.

We are still in the cycle of the moon, and we're not yet in the time where the sun and the moon are equal in size like they used to be. Instead, they are on a journey and the moon is constantly developing and changing.

Therefore, when we daven the half-*Hallel* on Rosh Chodesh, we are recognizing that obviously it's a celebration, it's a *moed*, you wear special clothing. We eat special meals; we daven at special times.[1] Yet with all these specialties we still say half-*Hallel* because we have to realize the beauty of patience. We have to be able to accept the fact that we're not there yet and not fight against it.

Personally, I think that this is also the idea of Yom HaZikaron occurring before Yom Ha'atzmaut. Yom Ha'atzmaut could be a very dangerous day, were we to think that we'd reached the end and that the story is over. It is very scary that we might look at Yom Ha'atzmaut as the *geulah*, because it's not true.

The answer is that we can only relate to Yom Ha'atzmaut in a healthy way if we also internalize Yom HaZikaron, both in terms of its pain and its demands. It is so painful that, no matter where we look, everyone is experiencing Yom HaZikaron. It is so painful, a tearing of the heart, and it's also a demand. A demand to realize that it's not enough to remember if it's not also going to become an active memory, of realizing that we are exactly like those soldiers. We are the same people, we grew up in the same land, and they are demanding of us not just to remember their story, but to also live differently because of them and through them. All the names written in our *siddurim* that we daven for every day, and all the people that we've lost throughout the journey of building the Land of Israel demand of us daily that we not just remember them as from the past, but as something that has significance for the present. It needs to be something that we look at and we understand that we are not allowed to just be normal anymore, and we can no longer be regular people. That's what Yom Hazikaron is teaching us in preparation for Yom Ha'atzmaut: Don't look at Yom Ha'atzmaut as the ending because it is the beginning. It is a beautiful start, it's an amazing start, but it's a start.

We should be *zocheh* at the end of this week to really dance on Yom Ha'atzmaut. To recognize that our feet need to stamp on the land, they need to press on the land, they need to make the land grow, and they need to realize that we need to be planted in this land. I think that the

---

1   Rav Yair has a 5:45 *vatikin* minyan at the hotel every Rosh Chodesh.

combination of all of this puts us into a very unique week that's getting us ready for the celebration, the demand, and the dedication of remembering every one of our soldiers. We need to demand of ourselves to live them and to internalize them. To have them not only as memory for ourselves, but a recognition of the beauty of Eretz Yisrael and the people of Eretz Yisrael and the need to keep making it grow and flourish.

Parashat Acharei Mot—Kedoshim

YOU CAN LIVE ANY GAME WITHOUT ME

> "The real me is more than I."

OPENING QUESTIONS

1. How would you define *kedushah*?
2. Who is a person you think truly lives a life of *kedushah*?
3. What is the difference between *taharah* and *kedushah*?
4. What is your advice to enable a person to become *kadosh*?
5. Why do you think we mourn for Rabbi Akiva's students for thirty-three out of the forty-nine days that prepare us for *Matan Torah*?

LEARNING CONVERSATION

Parashat Kedoshim, *Parashat Emor* and in general *Sefer Vayikra* place a lot of emphasis on the concept of *kedushah*. Obviously, in *Parashat Kedoshim*, we speak about the idea of *kedushah*.

Often, we say a word so many times that we don't even think about it. I want to use a short *Sefat Emet* to develop this concept of the idea and lifestyle of *kedushah*. The parashah of *Kedoshim* opens up and says, "דבר אל כל עדת בני ישראל ואמרת אלהם קדשים תהיו כי קדוש אני ד׳ אלקיכם—Speak to the whole Israelite community and say to them: You shall be holy, for I, the Lord, your God, am holy."[1] The literal translation of the *pasuk* is that God demands of the Jewish people "*kedoshim tihiyu*—Be holy," and

---

1   *Vayikra* 19:2.

this is because "*Ki kadosh Ani*—I am Holy." There are a few questions we need to ask and the first is, What is *kedushah*? The second is, what does this command and the reason for it have to do with one another? Rather Hashem should say that if you are holy, you will fix the world or you will be happy, or you won't be selfish, and you will be able to realize that you are not the only person in the world. What does it mean that you—Am Yisrael—should be holy because I (Hashem) am Holy? It's as if someone came over to you and said, "Be a great basketball player because I'm a great basketball player." But what if I don't want to be a basketball player, and I don't have the talents to be a basketball player; and just because this person is a basketball player doesn't mean anything about me and what I want to be. The third question is, Why does the *pasuk* switch from plural in the task given to Am Yisrael to singular at the end. If you ever look at the word *kedushah* in relation to people, it's always in plural of *kedoshim*. The *pasuk* could have read "קדוש תהיה כי קדוש אני." A lot of times the Torah speaks in singular to the individual, but it's not written like that here. "*Ki kadosh*" in singular refers only to Hashem. If you look in *Shemoneh Esreh* also we say, "אתה קדוש ושמך קדוש וקדושים בכל יום יהללוך—Hashem is Holy, His name is Holy, and we are holy." There is never a place that you will find holiness referred to in the singular when it is talking about people. It never happens—only in relation to Hashem himself. Through the third question, I want to develop the issue of *kedushah* and then end with a *Sefat Emet*.

That little focus on the difference between the command of *kedoshim*, being holy, and the reason of "*Ki kadosh Ani*—because I am Holy," is significant. We live in times where our lives center around our accomplishments. Our success is *our* success. "Ours," meaning: it's mine. Therefore, most high schoolers' focus is on university, because that is where they'll get *their* degree. University is incredible and amazing, but it's a little bit detrimental when someone living through their teenage years only focuses on the one issue of what his job will be in the future. *B'ezrat Hashem*, yes, you will have a job, but is that the only thing that you are thinking about? I was *zocheh* one time to be in a city in North America, and a second grader walked over to me, and he said, "Rav Yair, should I go to Harvard or to Yale?" I looked at the second grader, and for me it was a little bit scary. I think the question a second grader should be asking is, "Why was Avraham Avinu chosen?" And then they could focus on how this will make them a better businessman. But it can't be that the focus is my job because then you have to be very focused on yourself. The fear and the danger of what happens is that so many people live the life of *kadosh* but they forget *kedoshim*. The focus of *kedushah* in human beings is you will never reach it alone, no matter what you do and matter where you go because *kedushah* does not belong to the individual. The only singular that could be holy is Hashem. We can only reach *kedushah* if we realize that we cannot accomplish goals of *kedushah* on our own.

My wife, Tanya, asked the most brilliant question: Why would we decide to mourn during *sefirat ha'omer* for Rabbi Akiva's students? These days should be happy days preparing for the Torah, but instead of that we are mourning over the students of Rabbi Akiva. Yes, the experience was painful, but how does that trump the *simchah* of preparing for the Torah? I think Tanya's answer was incredible. Her answer was that if the Torah becomes self-centered, it is the destruction of the Torah. The two are not separate things, but they are linked to each other. The link between them is that if you are living a Torah that is focused on *your* growth, then that is what will destroy *Matan Torah*. The mourning isn't really mourning, but it's a mindset. It's a learning process, and it means realizing that the Torah is not medicine. You have to realize that Torah can also be destructive, and it can be selfish, and therefore we need to realize that though we're learners, we are not learned people. This means that if we are not affected, changing, or developed by out learning, then our Torah becomes destructive. We are not mourning for the students of Rabbi Akiva, but rather, we are mourning over the idea that the Torah is something that could become *kadosh* for me, and not *kedushah* for us.

The third question was why did we transition from plural to singular? The answer is that the message is if you want to reach *kedushah*, you need to realize that I, the individual, am singular and you in the singular will always destroy. You will never build anything on your own. That is the definition of *kedushah*.

Our second question was, what is the connection between the idea of *kedoshim* and the concept of "*ki kadosh Ani.*" The *Sefat Emet* says, "כי איך יכול ב"ו להתקדש." He says that the problem isn't Hashem's reason, the problem is His command for us to be holy. What does that mean to be *kedoshim tihiyu*, that you should be holy? You eat breakfast, right? You eat lunch, right? You eat dinner, right? Well so does a cow!

A cow also eats breakfast, lunch, and dinner. You are also excited that you have a few friends? Well, so do the cows! So, the question really is, how can you be holy? His answer is, "רק להיות הרצון והשתוקקות לזה."[2] You are right; you can't be *kadosh*. But what makes you different from a cow is not who you are, but what you want. What you want will affect you and it will change you. The deepest idea that the *Sefat Emet* develops regarding *kedushah* is that it's intangible; it's not an action but a mind-set of what you want. You will not be Rav Kook until you want to be. You will not be Avraham Avinu until you want to be. What makes you different and what makes you *kadosh* is the world that you want.

To summarize the issue of *kedushah*, there are two ideas. The first is that what we want is what makes you *kadosh*. The second is that *kedushah* is the understanding that alone, you will always fail. We discussed that with the students of Rabbi Akiva and with the ties that we are in with Yom Yerushalayim, Yom Ha'Atzmaut, Yom HaZikaron, and Lag Ba'omer that all these unique days are preparing us for *Matan Torah*. They are saying that anyone who fought in 1948 in the Israeli War of Independence knew that they were doing what they were doing only so that someone else could enjoy it. Even though they didn't enjoy it, it is what helped them gain control of the land. People who realize that alone you are a failure are the ones that build society in the world. Then we saw how the *Sefat Emet* made a connection between command and reason. *Ki kadosh Ani*—Because I am holy means I just want to be like Hashem. You never will be like Hashem, but if Hashem created the world, then stop only worrying about yourself and start creating.

---

2   *Sefat Emet, Vayikra, Kedoshim* 2.

If Hashem has patience, then you should want to have patience. The *ratzon*, desire, to be like Hashem is the essence of *kedushah*.

My berachah as we enter *Parashat Kedoshim* is that we should all focus on the issue of *kedushah*—the *kedushah* of the idea that I don't want to build alone, and the *kedushah* of the idea that I want big things because what makes someone big is that they want something big.

LIVING THE LEARNING

Write ten commandments of your own that will stop you from thinking about or trying to achieve greatness on your own.

Parashat Emor / Lag Ba'omer

THE HEALING SUN

THERE IS A PASUK in our parashah that is developed at the beginning of *Masechta Berachot* that can help us internalize the concept of *kehunah* and maybe even get into the depth of what Lag Ba'omer is. The *pasuk* has three words, and it discusses the process of *taharah*. It says, "ובא השמש וטהר—As soon as the sun sets, he shall be clean."[1]

The concept underpinning this *pasuk* is that it is possible for someone to transform. Admittedly, we don't really understand what *tum'ah* and *taharah* are with regard to routine life. Nevertheless, a person who is *tamei* cannot go into the Beit Hamikdash, whereas a person who is *tahor* can, and the transition from one to the other is a major transformation. When you are *tamei* you are removed, and when you are *tahor* you are relevant. But what causes this transformation?

The *pasuk* says that the one thing that transforms a person from his place of removal to his place of relevance is sunset. The obvious question is, "Ribbono Shel Olam, seriously?" What is so difficult about the sun setting? It sets on teenagers, on adults, and on babies. You don't have to do anything for it to happen. What does that mean that in order for someone to transform themselves, the main thing is for the sun to set? In fact, on a practical level, if someone is *tamei* for one day, then the only thing that is a necessity is for them to do is to wait for sunset. So, what happens in that moment of sunset that has the ability to transform a person?

---

1   *Vayikra* 22:7.

The answer might be that when the sun sets on you, it shows you your place. It gives you the awareness that there are so many things that you are not able to do, and that realization is the greatest transformation—the realization that you are not able to do everything. In fact, it is this realization that there are things that are bigger and greater, and that there are things that you can't fix, which is exactly why you are going to become a fixer.

Interestingly, the more we think that we can do everything, the more that we start idolizing ourselves. Contrasting this, the more that we recognize the sun is setting, and that it is greater and bigger than us and that we can't control the sun, the more we will be enabled to become free if we internalize that experience.

For Kohanim, the main thing that they experience is the eating of the *terumah*. You think what makes the Kohanim great is that they are active, but what is *terumah*? *Terumah* represents the fact that the food they eat is dependent on others. The greatest element is that they recognize that they are not able to perform their service without assistance from others.

Now, when we look at Lag Ba'omer, we see that Rabbi Shimon Bar Yochai thought that the world was something that we have to look down upon, and so he burned it. Suddenly, he realized after twelve years of being in the cave that the world is not something that's supposed to be minimized, but it's supposed to teach you your place. The world shows you that you are dependent, that you cannot go beyond the world, and that you need to stay involved. And just because you know Torah doesn't mean you have permission to escape from the world. The message of Rabbi Akiva and his students is that they were elevating themselves to a level that the normality of life became a nuisance to them.

As such, the goal of Lag Ba'omer, in preparation for *Matan Torah*, is to realize that the words of Hashem are written on parchment. Parchment is a cow. This means that we rely on a cow to write a *Sefer Torah*.

We need to recognize that the more we think that we can do without the world, and the more we disassociate from our responsibilities in life, we actually become the opposite of the sunsets ability to transform; we become the opposite of *terumah*. We become the opposite of Rabbi

Shimon Bar Yochai teaching us that the world is not random, but is rather Hashem's message that we should understand the need to support each others.

We are supposed to embrace the world that assists us in realizing that we need food, we need water, and we need people. The more we think that we can elevate ourselves, the more destructive we become. The more we realize that we can relate to the level of needing the world, the more we can start to fall in love with the idea that Hashem wants a world that we're in love with and not a world that we step on.

Parashat Behar

REAL NEW, FEEL NEW

PARASHAT BEHAR teaches us about *shemittah*, the Sabbatical year. Every seventh year, we stop planting, and we stop changing the land. It's very similar to Shabbat. We work for six days, and on the seventh day we accept that reality is perfect. During *shemittah* too, we accept and feel perfection.

The idea of *shemittah* is that we recognize that Hashem is involved in the land. But the *Sefat Emet* is bothered by the mitzvah of *shemittah*. He says that Hashem brought us to Eretz Yisrael, so why should we need to remember every seven years that Hashem gave us the land? It's like if a couple gets married then wants to remember that they got married, so they redo the ceremony again every seven years.

Really, *shmittah* isn't teaching us that Hashem gave us the land, but it's giving us a new understanding of what it means to have the land. The *Sefat Emet* says, "וזה מצות השמטה, שניתן לבני ישראל הארץ מחדש."[1] The idea of *shemittah* is not recognizing that Hashem gave us the land sometime in the past, but realizing that Hashem is giving us the land every single day, *michadash*, like new. You need to be in the land to realize that Hashem is renewing the land all the time.

What does this really mean? I think that we have to understand what renewal is all about. I had the opportunity to go to Toronto for three years. I came back to Jerusalem, and everything was new. But that's not the renewal of *shemittah*. During *shemittah*, you can't make anything new! So *shemittah*'s idea of "new" is that you can look at the same thing

---

1   *Sefat Emet, Vayikra, Behar* 16:2.

differently. It's that you look at the same land with new eyes. It's that you look at the same story in Tanach with new eyes. You're looking at the same information that might not actually be new, but it is new because we're looking at it differently.

To renew a relationship, you don't have to change it, but you have to see it from a different perspective. You can learn *Masechta Berachot* seven times, but it will be different the seventh time than the first time. *Shemittah* challenges us to open it seven times and learn it differently each time. The *chiddush* of *shemittah* is that we have an obligation to realize that we need to change the way we deal with the land on a daily basis. If you're walking in Jerusalem daily in the Old City, maybe walk slowly. If you're walking into your home, maybe realize the privilege you have to walk into your home. It's the same family; it's the same home; it's the same street. But if you walk in each time with a renewed perspective, it'll make you feel different.

We daven the same *tefillah* every day. So maybe if we pause to think about today's experiences, then the *tefillah* will be new. It's easy to do new things. But can we do the same thing in a different way, with a new perspective?

My berachah as we enter *Parashat Behar* is that we should realize that we need to change our perspective each day. Each day of *sefirat ha'omer* has a different *sefirah*, a different perspective. We should merit to have the ability to understand that the people that we're closest to are the ones that we need to renew our relationships with constantly.

Parashat Bechukotai

PLACES MATTER

THERE ARE THREE WORDS at the beginning of the parashah that I want to use in order to understand both Lag Ba'omer and *Sefer Vayikra* differently. Our parashah opens up, "אם בחוקותי תלכו—if, in My laws, you will walk."[1]

A lot of commentaries struggle with the link between the words *chukim*, laws, and *telechu*, you will walk. This is because *chukim*, laws, are intellectual. We conceptualize laws with our brains. So, why doesn't the parashah say that we should listen to the laws or learn the laws? Why are we linking laws to walking?

The *Sefat Emet* tries to understand this relationship. He says that the real will of a person is not measured by what he learned, but where he goes. You know more about yourself from where you go and what you do, than from what you learn, think or want. For example, people know that they want to be happy, that they want to have a relationship with Hashem. But if you're not working—or walking in a metaphorical sense—toward that goal, that's not the real you! Where you are reveals who you are. If someone is constantly in bed watching Netflix, even though he says he wants to be productive, he's not "walking the walk." Your steps and the direction in which you're walking reveal your true desires. Where you walk is who you are.

As we approach Lag Ba'omer, we've been mourning for thirty days over the death of Rabbi Akiva's students. How could these scholars

---

1   *Vayikra* 26:3.

have fallen into such a dark place? Twenty-four thousand leaders of the Jewish people were gone!

We can perhaps understand this tragedy through what Rabbi Akiva was teaching his students and what they failed to grasp. Rabbi Akiva's famous teaching is "ואהבת לרעך כמוך, זה כלל גדול בתורה"—You shall love your neighbor as yourself: Rabbi Akiva says: 'This is a fundamental [all-inclusive] principle of the Torah.'"[2] It sounds simple, but it's actually complicated. Sometimes when we think of a *klal gadol*, a great idea, we become more removed from the little details in life. People who are dealing with the biggest questions in the world aren't dealing with the details. The more they deal with the details, the more they become removed from their feet.

When I was in Otniel, I always saw Rav Re'em, the Rosh Yeshiva, take out the garbage after lunch. He was the Rosh Yeshiva! There's no reason he should have been taking out the garbage! That's the custodian's job, right!? Rav Re'em taught me that even though you just learned Gemara for five hours, it could potentially be a dangerous experience. The more we get involved in the *klal gadol*, we sometimes remove ourselves from the small details.

Lag Ba'omer is such a spiritual experience, but we can't get lost in the *klal gadol*. If a person forgets his responsibilities and commitments while getting over-involved in lofty concepts, he's doomed. We can learn such incredible things but end up losing it all if we don't pay attention to the small details that are the foundation of those ideas. The parashah is asking us if we're involved in action, because action is what enables the *klal gadol* to exist.

This is *Sefer Vayikra*. It's a book that taught us about *telechu*. It taught us all the fine details of *shechitah* and sprinkling the blood, etc. We get bored with the details. There were no stories or revelations; it is mostly laws. *Sefer Bereishit* is so much more interesting! But if we can't get involved with the details, then everything falls apart.

---

2   *Rashi* on *Vayikra* 19:18.

My berachah as we enter the next part of *sefirat ha'omer* is that we realize that in order to reach the mountain, we first need to fall in love with the valley. If you learn to love the valley of *sefirat ha'omer*, you will appreciate the mountain of Shavuot so much more. We should merit to fall in love with the fine details to appreciate the *klal gadol* so much more.

Parashat Behar-Bechukotai

MULTITASKING

WE REACH THE END of *Sefer Vayikra* with *Parashat Behar-Bechukotai*. The question that arises is what is *Sefer Vayikra* all about? What is the secret of this book? It is very different from all the other ones. It's very different from the stories of *Bereishit*, the redemption of *Shemot*, and the preparation for Israel in *Bamidbar* and *Devarim*. It is primarily about *korbanot* and *tum'ah* and *taharah*. That is pretty much what it deals with. So, what is the significance of *Sefer Vayikra*?

Maybe through three words of this parashah we can understand it. The words are "אם בחקתי תלכו—If you follow My laws."[1] The *Sefat Emet* explains that the *chukim*, laws, are the mind because they're the highest part. Then he says that *telechu*, to follow or walk, refers to the feet which is the lowest part. The secret of the word *im*, if, is the condition that Hashem is giving us which is: Can you relate the mind, the vision, and the ideals to the reality of the feet, to the outside world, to the differences, to the complicated realities? The *Sefat Emet* says that is the idea of *Sefer Vayikra*.

Sefer Vayikra is more about the feet than it is about the mind. It is more about the animals than it is about the visionaries. It is more about *korbanot* than it is about stories. It is saying to us that the epicenter of Chumash is *Vayikra* which is in the middle. It's saying to us that the *telechu* is not minimizing the ideal, but it's defining the ideal. The ideal is only as great as one can relate to it and correlate it to reality.

---

1   *Vayikra* 26:3.

184

My berachah, as we reach the end of *Sefer Vayikra*, is that we should be prepared to deal with the world of the feet. It's about realizing that the *telechu* is not minimizing the ideal, but it's giving the ideal its ideal. This means that it is not just some elevated concept to remain above, and it's not just about everything going on course. It means that I can deal with things when they go out of course, when things go the opposite way, and when they go to the place where we least expected.

Just to add a joke—sometimes when people have relationships there is a concept called "dumping," which is when you take another person from the highest and you throw them all the way down. According to *Sefer Vayikra*, there really is no such thing as dumping—there's only "upping." A person who looks at another person and thinks that the relationship isn't working is not throwing them down but throwing them up, as if they are saying that you have more to build for your next relationship, for your next connection, for your next opportunity, and for your next ability. So yes, we've been thrown down in this Corona-era, but it's not in order to reminisce over what was. It's in order to realize that the *telechu* and the reality is something that is defining the ideal, and it's not just minimizing the ideal.

THE THIRD MONTH FOR TORAH

B'EZRAT HASHEM we are nearing Shavuot, and there are two things to focus on. The first is the name of the *sefer*, *Bamidbar*.

We know that the desert is where we received the Torah, and the name for the desert in Hebrew is *midbar*, which comes from the word *dibur*, speech. The place that Hashem gave us the Torah is called the *midbar*, and through this, it defines the message of the Torah.

The second thing is that, in *Shemot*, we open up the story of *maamad Har Sinai*, and the first two words are "בחודש השלישי—On the third new moon."[1] These two words are the entrance code into understanding not just when the Torah was given, but why it was given. In the Jewish calendar, we basically have two main months. We have *chodesh harishon*, the first month, which is where Hashem chose us, and *chodesh hashevi'i*, the seventh month, which is where we choose Hashem. Our question is, Why couldn't Hashem have given the Torah in the first month and taught us that the idea of the Torah being like the first month is about Hashem choosing us? Or why couldn't he have given it in the seventh month and said that we are choosing Hashem through our Torah learning? What is the idea of *chodesh hashlishi*? Why was it given in the third month?

In answering this question, we need to ponder the secret of the number three which I think may help us recognize the secret that the Torah is trying to teach us.

We know that we say every day, "Hashem is One," which means that Hashem's presence is felt in a world with no conflict, no tension, no

---

1   *Shemot* 19:1.

problems, and no difficulties. All of us are trying to search for that world, the perfect world. We think that's the ideal. The perfect world is found in *chodesh harishon*. That is the month of Hashem that we are searching and yearning for. After one is two.

The *Maharal* teaches that there's no other word where we add a *mem* when we multiply it. *Shalosh* doesn't end with a *mem, arbah* doesn't end with a mem, *chamesh* doesn't end with a *mem*. The letter *mem* is plural and is in the world of multiplication.

We can clearly see this idea in the number two: *sh'nayim*. Two is where we multiply, which is the idea of *p'ru u'revu*. The number two is about conflict and where things have tension. Things are different than one, because the *echad* is complete whereas the *sh'nayim* has tension. Left wing and right wing. *Chiloni* and chareidi. North and South. That is the idea of the number. The word is *sh'nayim*, which ends with a *mem*, meaning that it exists in the world of multiplication, or in other words, differences.

On one hand, Hashem is complete and the world is incomplete. So, we think let's just leave the world and run away to the world of Hashem. Let's leave the problems and just run away to perfection. Let's build yeshivas that are perfect and that don't have windows and whose doors are locked up. They look at Hashem in the book, but they can't see the world of multiplication and differences. They can't see the missiles and they can't feel the pain. They can't see the brokenness.

Mori v'rabi, Rav Re'em, says that a yeshiva without windows is a *teivah* that destroys the world. You need to see the conflict and you need to see the tension. But for what? Why do I want to see the tension? Hashem says it's because you can take the problems and make something new. You can take the problems and demand of yourself to be creative and an advocate of new creation. Hashem is saying I didn't give you the world to replicate. I didn't give you a world to duplicate. I didn't give you a world so you could go backward, but I gave you a world to go forward. Take the conflict, address the conflict, see the conflict, internalize the conflict, and realize that Hashem is asking to sing a new *niggun* on Shavuot, during the third month.

You've seen Hashem and now you've seen the world. It is now time to demand of yourself to look at the world, not to step backward, but instead, to move forward. You need to demand of yourself, and the people around you, and your family, to build not what was, but what will be. This is why we have three Batei Mikdashot.

The first Beit Hamikdash had an *Aron* and revealed God. It was perfect, but we were bad.

In the second Beit Hamikdash there was no *Aron*. We thought we would try and learn Torah and believed that respecting others didn't matter, that we didn't need to deal with the world. The second Beit Hamikdash was about realizing that we need to demand of ourselves to look at the world and not hate the world or differences.

Bayit Shlishi is not called Beit Hamikdash Harishon. Now you've seen the baseless hatred and if you don't realize that people see the difference as something that is confronting you and not completing you then you'll never get Bayit Shlishi. We need Bayit Shlishi so much, but we first need to understand the word *shlishi*. We need to internalize the idea that it's not about looking backward to what was. Instead, it is about realizing that getting back to Yerushalayim gives us a new image, meaning Mashiach rebuilding the Temple with the Third Beit Hamikdash.

Yom Ha'atzmaut gave us a physical land. Yom Yerushalayim gave us the spiritual component. And Am Yisrael was torn between these two—the ones who love Yom Yerushalayim and diminish Yom Ha'atzmaut, and the ones that love Yom Ha'atzmaut and diminish Yom Yerushalayim. It is only with these two that we can build Shavuot. Nissan showed us the ability of Hashem, followed by Yom Yerushalayim in Iyar which taught us the peak of our ability. Now, we must realize that Hashem wants us to be the ones to build and that's why the Torah is given in the *midbar*. The differences can only become a creation through a conversation.

We all know that the greatest and highest level between husband and wife is when they are able to converse about their differences. It is then that they are able to realize how they are built in their very nature and how they speak and think differently from one another.

The berachah to Am Yisrael, as we're entering into *chodesh* Sivan, is that we should be *zocheh*, *b'ezrat Hashem*, to not be afraid of tension. We must let the differences speak to each other like *Moreinu v'Rabbeinu*

Rav Froman teaches: If you take one side, and another side, you could see that they are different. But if you bring them together, they make a noise, and it creates a clap, it makes sound, music and excitement that we're all in need of.

Parashat Naso

JUST WALK BESIDE ME

PARASHAT NASO BEGINS by instructing us that we have to count Shevet Levi.

Interestingly, the Leviim not only become an issue in *Sefer Bamidbar*, but they actually become the centerpiece in the building of Am Yisrael and the foundation for preparing the entrance into Eretz Yisrael. But what is it about Shevet Levi that gives them this position?

We have to first remember that before Levi was a tribe, Levi was an individual. If we go back all the way to the beginning, when Levi was born and look at the name that he was given, we can learn about the essence of the tribe.

At the end of *Bereishit*, *perek chaf-tet*, Leah seeks a stronger, more loving relationship with Yaakov. When Reuven was born, she said that Hashem could see that she was struggling, and when Shimon is born, she describes how she could hear that she was someone who is hated. She was searching for love and companionship, and when Levi was born she said, "עתה הפעם ילוה אישי—This time my husband will become attached to me."[1] But what is the meaning of this *pasuk*?

As should be clear, the word *yilaveh* is the basis of the name "Levi" which means to accompany and to be someone who is willing to walk next to another person. It is a person who is willing, on a certain level, to be the side note, a person who is willing to be the one to listen, even if they don't have all the answers. This is what Leah is really saying, "I just want to escort. That's all I want; for someone to be happy in my success

---

1   *Bereishit* 29:34.

190

and for someone to be willing to participate and watch the growth that I am going through."

Later, in *Parashat Korach*, Shevet Levi is defined according to what Hashem says to Aharon—that they'll escort you and they'll serve you. That becomes the definition of this individual child, which is derived from the fact that Leah just wants someone to walk next to her.

If we think about this on a superficial level, why would Levi ever want to do such a thing, especially in the light of the Modern Era where it's all about success and thriving. There is this whole mindset that second place is last place, that you have to be on the top, and if you're not on the top then you're on the bottom. So, what was so exciting the Leviim to just be an escort? They just who got to sing on the outskirts of the Beit Hamikdash but didn't get to go preform the service or go into the *Kodesh Hakodashim*. The Leviim protected the walls of the Beit Hamikdash, but they didn't get to sacrifice *korbanot*. Why would someone be willing to live this kind of lifestyle?

The answer is that Shevet Levi is aware of the fact that personal success is also personal sadness. The more we succeed and the more we develop, the more we often don't feel we need anyone else. We become totally independent while, at the same time, we become extremely lonely.

Levi understood that success involves danger. He understood that success could cause you to become elitist, to become judgmental, to become belittling, and to become competitive toward others and dismissive of others. Given this, Levi provides us with a new approach to what real Judaism is about. Real Judaism is about recognizing that it's not a goal-oriented life, but a relationship-oriented life.

My *abba* and *imma* always say that when you say something good about a child to his parents, the parents will never become jealous of their child because they are so connected in such a relationship that they rejoice in the success of their child. But all this is dependent on the fact that they are aware of the relationship and what it means to be connected and linked to others and not against others. This is what causes joy, and it is what causes excitement instead of competitiveness. It is what causes relaxation, instead of stress. It is when I am able to realize that someone else's success is so much more fun than mine, and now I get to enjoy watching the world become better. I recognize through looking at their success that I am not the be-all and end-all, and therefore I can start enjoying the world instead of fighting it.

I think this is why Shevet Levi is the preparation for Eretz Yisrael. Eretz Yisrael is not a land that is searching for leaders. Instead, it is a land that is searching for relationships. Sometimes we speak so much about the concept of leadership that we actually, without even being aware of it, cause competitiveness and a feeling of isolation from society. We convince ourselves we need to be better in order to be happy. In response to this, *Sefer Bamidbar* teaches us, through Shevet Levi, that it's not like that. It teaches us that Shevet Levi carried the vessels, and they didn't do anything with them, but they were happy to be part of the building. They didn't have to build alone, and they didn't have to fight against others in order to feel good about themselves.

Considering the period of time that we are living in right now, where thousands of rockets from Hamas are being shot into Israel, and children aren't in school and are hiding in the bomb shelters, we realize that Am Yisrael needs a society that is able to look at each other and say that I am not looking for my safety in order for me to survive. Instead, I am davening for your safety and I am davening for your success. That will make all of us realize that we are never ever alone, and we don't need to live in a world of competition, but rather we can live in a world of joy and *simchah*.

SMALLER IS CLOSER

B'EZRAT HASHEM in Eretz Yisrael we are in *Parashat Behaalotecha*, and outside of Eretz Yisrael, we are in *Parashat Naso*, but we will continue with the story of the parashah in Eretz Yisrael. We know that in this week's parashah there is a famous challenge for Aharon. When we look at the end of *Parashat Behaalotecha*, Aharon sees all of the *nesi'im*, princes, giving these great *korbanot* and sacrificing thousands and thousands of animals. Seeing this, he gets very frustrated because he suddenly feels like he is unimportant in comparison to what the *nesi'im* are giving. Hashem then tells Aharon that his contribution is really even greater than the *korbanot*, as he has the privilege to light the *Menorah*. Yet, there is difficulty in understanding Hashem's response to Aharon, because in reality, lighting a candle is not that difficult, special, or expensive. For the *nesi'im* to have brought this vast amount of copper, gold, and animals, it might have cost millions upon millions of *shekels*. It was an incredible statement to the world. We know that lighting a match, and then putting it to a candle takes under ten seconds. In addition, candle wax is only three *shekels*, and if one wants to use olive oil it might cost upward of ten *shekels*. Therefore, what Aharon was doing by lighting the candles was inexpensive, not difficult, and it failed to reflect Aharon's great qualities and abilities. What is so unique then about the fact that Aharon got to light the candles?

One possible answer is that there is a big difference between closeness and being a servant who is distant. The farther that someone is, the greater the need he has to do big things. The more that a relationship lacks, the more it is measured by the quantity and difficulty of the things that the other person does.

I remember in the army, in order to become a soldier, we had to do very big and complicated things in the beginning as training. We had to carry stretchers and run for eight kilometers, all while operating on three hours of sleep a night. These actions took us outside of who we were, and we were definitely not natural soldiers. One has to do these big transformative acts, and only then does he get to be a soldier. But what happened afterward? After one goes through great tribulations and training, throwing grenades, shooting, etc., he gets to stand for around eight months in a single lookout post, guarding a single mountain. One day, I remember thinking to myself, "Yair, what in the world did you train for? You were doing big things, and now you are spending all day standing at a single post?" The need to have made those huge sacrifices and partake in the crazy activities was because I was not yet a soldier. Once I became a soldier, my actions were measured not by quantity, but by the fact that I was able to do something unordinary and mundane, like watching a single mountain for eleven hours straight each day. I think this is what Hashem was saying to Aharon HaKohen.

Hashem is saying to Aharon that the *nesi'im* are doing big things because they are servants, but that Aharon is unlike them; he is special like a child. In order for a child to connect and build a relationship with his father, he only needs to do simple things. Their shared experiences only have to be simple, yet the father and child both experience the relationship in such special ways, because their actions show that they are close and connected.

We are currently getting more and more involved in the coronavirus pandemic, and it is becoming more difficult and complicated. I often see that people are trying to plan big things online and are always looking for something else to do. On Yom Ha'atzmaut they organize massive flag-making virtual calls, on Yom Yerushalayim they are building cities, and on Lag Ba'omer they host virtual fires, etc. Yet, maybe the idea of our time is to realize that if we are really close, we can connect to each other in simpler ways. We can say something nice to someone. We do not need all these virtual realities and additions because they prove not that we are close but rather that we are distant.

Parashat Behaalotecha

THINK BIG

FROM THE BEGINNING of *Sefer Bamidbar*, we're dealing with one central issue: Taking a nation—a former slave nation, that lacks order and organization—and getting them ready to walk together into a new land, Eretz Yisrael. That is the storyline from the beginning until now. We open our parashah with one of the most difficult parshiyot in the Torah. Suddenly, out of nowhere, we say, "בהעלתך את הנרת"—When you mount the lamps."[1] The idea is that it's obviously speaking about the *Menorah*, but why here? We already spoke about the building of the *Mishkan* in *Shemot*, and there we read and were told about the *Menorah*. Do we discuss the *Mizbei'ach*? No. Do we discuss the *Aron*? No. So what is the reason that, out of nowhere, we are now discussing the *Menorah*?

Rashi gives an answer that it is part of the preparation for entering into the Land of Israel. The *nesi'im* brought *korbanot*, and Aharon was embarrassed that he was not a *nasi* of a tribe. Consequently, Hashem consoled him by telling him that he has the *Menorah*. Moshe says to Aharon, "שלך גדולה מהן—Your part is of greater importance than theirs."[2] Admittedly, the answer is beautiful. But within the context of preparing to enter into Eretz Yisrael, what is the significance of the *Menorah* appearing?

The key word for the *Menorah* is *behaalotecha*. The idea of the *Menorah* is realizing that there's a very big danger in what has happened in *Sefer Bamidbar*. During *Sefer Bamidbar*, all the pieces of Am Yisrael were given specific jobs. Reuven is here, Shimon is there. Ephraim has this color

---

1   *Bamidbar* 8:2.
2   *Rashi, Bamidbar* 8:2.

flag. And Menashe has this colored flag. We saw all the tribes get their placements. What happens is, you suddenly lose the love of life. You lose the love of fresh and new. You lose the love from something exciting and something that's going to be not just regular. Every single *nasi* brought the same exact *korban*—which represents the climax of organization. There is something so strong about it, but also so dangerous. That danger is that we'll forget to yearn, excel, and to want big things. And that is where the *Menorah* comes in.

The *Menorah* reminds us that, however organized you are, and however systematic you are, and however consistent you are, you cannot let it be an exchange for your desire. Do not let it prevent your big goals and dreams. The fire goes up no matter what, because it is yearning to go somewhere bigger. You must think big!

There's a famous video going around now of thousands of people that went to Lod. They left their comfort and left their consistent lives all because they were able to think big. There are families that were petrified, and children who are crying at night scared. We are now bringing in all the people from the Golan, Yerushalayim, Kiryat Shemoneh, and Ma'aleh HaChamishah. They are all coming to Lod and saying that we didn't come to Eretz Yisrael to think small. Instead, we came to think like the *Menorah*.

The berachah to Am Yisrael, *b'ezrat Hashem*, is that we should be *zocheh* to have real *nachat*, real comfort, but that we shouldn't let ourselves think small. Instead, we should open our eyes to the story of Am Yisrael and learn the history of prime ministers like Menachem Begin. We should be able to learn about all the greatness of big thinkers who are the definition of "*behaalotecha et haneirot.*"

Ultimately, it is not enough to just have organized Eretz Yisrael. Instead, we need to also recognize that Eretz Yisrael is searching for people who are seeking to expand themselves. We should be *zocheh* for that berachah to give us unlimited vision.

A LAND OF FRUITS

PARASHAT SHELACH is a parashah that has had a seemingly endless number of books written about it. People commonly ask, "What happened? How did this disaster occur?" But before answering this question, it is important for us to look at the types of people that were sent. The Torah specifies "שלח לך אנשים—Send men."[1] Send people that are very special, capable, and unique; people who are leaders. These people were not "random;" they were "קראי עדה מועד אנשי שם—Chosen in the assembly, men of repute."[2] These people were the actual symbol of greatness. Often, when we speak about the Meraglim, the spies, the people that were sent, we speak about their experience on a superficial level. As such, it is really important to remember "שלח לך אנשים," that the Torah is dealing with people who were not random, but instead, people that were Godly, aware, connected, and that walked hand-in-hand with Moshe Rabbeinu. This being considered, one might struggle to understand what was going on in the thought processes of these Meraglim. Of course, there really are a lot of options that could be valid answers to this question, but one that I particularly like might be something people may simply pass over.

When the Meraglim returned from Eretz Yisrael, they brought back fruits from the land. The description of the fruits is really the main focal point. The Torah mentions how they brought back the fruits, how many people held them, the kinds of fruit they brought, etc. It is interesting to note that this is also mentioned in the Mishnah in

---

1   *Bamidbar* 13:2.
2   *Bamidbar* 16:2.

Berachot 6:6, though the Mishnah does not explicitly mention the Meraglim. But what is so interesting and important about their bringing the fruits? The answer might be found in the pain that the Jews felt from the moment when they were leaving Mitzrayim. When Am Yisrael complained about having left Mitzrayim, they said "זכרנו את הדגה אשר נאכל במצרים חנם את הקשאים ואת האבטחים ואת החציר ואת הבצלים ואת השומים—We remember the fish that we used to eat free in Egypt, the cucumbers, the melons, the leeks, the onions, and the garlic."[3] They were speaking about vegetables, because they remembered Mitzrayim as a land with an abundance of vegetables. Therefore, the Meraglim brought back fruits from the Land of Israel to show that a change of climate would mean a change in lifestyle. Going to the Land of Israel was not about making aliyah; rather, it was about understanding and being aware of the differences that aliyah would entail. It was not about making it to the land, but rather about staying in the land. The Meraglim were trying to give over the message that the Land of Israel was the opposite of Mitzrayim.

Of course, this is not the only time this message was given over. The Torah later says, "הארץ אשר אתה בא שמה לרשתה לא כארץ מצרים הוא—The land that you are about to enter and possess is not like the land of Egypt."[4] Part of the definition of the Land of Israel is its contrast from Egypt. For example, the main source of water in Egypt is the Nile river, as opposed to the rain in Israel. Egypt was full of vegetables, and Israel is full of fruit. What do these contrasts really represent?

If one looks at Creation and Gan Eden with these notions in mind, it is increasingly clear that Gan Eden was all about fruit. The trees in Gan Eden provided fruit; there is no mention of vegetables. Man is supposed to go into this world and let go of the vegetables, while still holding onto the fruits. The vegetables are something that give a person an incredible connection to God, because they require a minimal amount of man's efforts. If there is rain, a *natural* occurrence, vegetables can grow. There is not a process that involves man's efforts; it

---

3   *Bamidbar* 11:5.
4   *Devarim* 11:10.

is not complicated. There are no *orlah* laws, as there are pertaining to fruit-bearing trees. The vegetables are nearly entirely handled by God. The idea of Gan Eden was that Hashem was trying to show man that the greatest paradise is when he understands the beauty of Hashem. This understanding of Hashem's beauty is only accomplished when man understands that the sustenance He gives, the fruits, requires man's efforts as well. For fruits to grow they need human supervision. They need involvement, security, help, and someone to take care of them. The idea of the Land of Israel that the Meraglim wanted to give over was that it was not like Mitzrayim. Eretz Yisrael was not a place where God would always reveal the answers. It was a place that would demand that you not wait for Hashem and that you try to understand Hashem. What were the Meraglim confused about? The confusion was about whether or not they believed the people were ready for this level, the level of Eretz Yisrael. The Meraglim knew that Eretz Yisrael was the goal; they understood what it symbolized, and what it would take to achieve this. Yet, they were not sure that a nation of slaves who were complaining about vegetables were really ready for the world of Eretz Yisrael and its fruits.

My berachah, as we look into this story of the Meraglim and we go into *Parashat Shelach*, is that we should recognize the greatness of Eretz Yisrael; recognize that it teaches us to live with Hashem, to walk with Hashem; and understand that Hashem believes in us.

Parashat Shelach

WE WANT TO GO UP

WHEN WE ENTER into *Parashat Shelach* there are so many big ideas to think about. The importance of leadership, the concept of Eretz Yisrael, and the idea of believing in yourself are all essential themes. One that I'd like to focus on is the conversation between the ten *meraglim* and the two *meraglim*. The ten *meraglim* came back and they showed Am Yisrael the fruits of the land. This was obviously meant to scare them. Am Yisrael had been used to the vegetables of Mitzrayim, which were easy to grow. Fruits, in contrast, are much more complicated, and when the Meragalim showed Am Yisrael that it was a land that would take a lot of toil and effort, it scared them. They gave them a whole list of the nations that were there, and they spoke about Amalek. They explained to them very logically that if you were thinking about things on a rational level, it would be a bad idea, for many reasons, to enter into the Land of Israel. It was in response to this rationale that Calev responded by saying, "*Aloh na'aleh*—For we shall surely overcome it."[1]

The Piaseczna Rebbe, in the Warsaw Ghetto in 1942, said that it was very weird what Calev chose to do.[2] The Meraglim spoke with so much rhetoric, so much rationale, and they provided so many intellectual explanations of why the people should not enter the land. On the other hand, Calev didn't even address any these points. He didn't say we would have Hashem on our side, or that we had Moshe Rabbeinu to assist us, or that we had all the greatest miracles that happened in the past which prove that we could overcome anything and anyone. He didn't even refer

---

1   *Bamidbar* 13:30.
2   *Aish Kodesh, Parshat Shelach.*

to the fact that Am Yisrael beat Amalek in the desert without an army. Calev could have said any of this, but he didn't. So, as the Piaseczna Rebbe asks, what does Calev's response of "*aloh na'aleh*" really mean?

The answer he gives can be found in his *sefer*, *Aish Kodesh*, but I think that there might be another answer for why Calev said "*aloh na'aleh*." If we go back to *Bereishit*, the last *nevuah* given to Yaakov Avinu on his way down to Mitzrayim was: "אנכי ארד עמך מצרימה ואנכי אעלך גם עלה," meaning that Hashem said, "I am going to go down with you, and I am going to go up and up with you."[3]

Admittedly, I'm not exactly sure where else we find this idea of "going up" twice, but it could be that Calev heard about this last *nevuah* which was given to Yaakov from tradition. It says in one phrase, "*anochi ered*," that when you go down it's one act. But then it says that when you're going up there are two levels. There is going up because you need to, and there is going up because you want to. Maybe Hashem was saying that you go down because you need to. Something must have gone wrong because no one wants to go down. This means that if you are going down it is because you needed to. Same too, when you're going up, sometimes it is because we need to due to image, responsibility, or an obligation. So, what was Hashem saying? He was telling Yaakov that My secret for you is to realize in life, that if you want to go up because you need to, then sometimes there's no point. You could reach the level of not just doing what you're doing out of obligation, but rather out of a perspective that I have a privilege, and an amazing present, that I am excited about. This could be what Calev was saying to the nation.

He was saying that you are all speaking about Eretz Yisrael on the level of necessity and that we need to go. When you speak about need, you speak about rationale, such as: Where will I have more financial success? Where is the better education? On the level of necessity, that is most always the conversation. Calev learned from the *nevuah* of Yaakov Avinu not go because he needed to but rather because he was excited to go. On the level of need, maybe the ten *meraglim* were right. Instead,

---

3   *Bereishit* 46:4.

I am simply going because it is a privilege, it's a present, and it is something that is so much greater than just my obligations. It is giving me the opportunities of connecting myself to Avraham, Yitzchak, and to Yaakov. It is giving myself the opportunity to elevate my own personal world. It gives me the relationship with Am Yisrael's past and future.

I often think that when we speak about the journey to Eretz Yisrael, saying "I am going to the army because Am Yisrael needs me," we have to change this into, "I am going to the army because I want to have the privilege of feeling Am Yisrael on my shoulders."

B'ezrat Hashem this should give us an opportunity to understand the depth of the words of Calev, the one who brought us back to Eretz Yisrael with the idea of wanting it, and not only from a sense of obligation.

Parashat Korach

GROUNDED

PARASHAT KORACH, my bar mitzvah parashah, contains many interesting things which are all centered around leadership and, specifically, Korach.

Significantly, one of the things that happened this week, which was almost a terrible tragedy, but which ended as an amazing miracle, was the fact that a huge sinkhole suddenly appeared in the parking lot of the Shaare Zedek Medical Center. Two cars even fell into the hole, but *baruch Hashem*, no one was wounded. Naturally, this event is something that we have to think about with regards to *Parashat Korach.*

As we know, there are many different punishments recorded in the Torah such as fires and floods. While we often associate these events as punishments where Hashem is punishing us, they are often something different: acts performed by Hashem to educate us. What this means is that through the punishment, Hashem is actually trying to reveal to us what the problem really is and what the causes are. And through this, we will be able to grow and change.

The punishment for Korach himself was that he was swallowed up by the ground. And the question that we have to ask ourselves is: How does this have anything to do with what Korach was saying? Korach was dealing with the question of leadership. Yet the reaction was that he was swallowed up by the earth. I think that if we take a deeper look at Korach's punishment, we can understand the problem of Korach's mindset.

There is a famous question that is asked regarding Korach: What is the link between the fact that *parashat tzitzit* immediately precedes the story of Korach? *Rashi*, according to the Midrash, brings a famous answer that Korach was saying to Moshe to make him look bad, "What

203

if we had a *beged* that was made only of *techelet*? Would we need to tie tzitzit for it?" What this suggests is that Korach was trying to show a new mindset of what should be the level of *kedushah*.

Significantly, the word *beged* comes from the word for "betrayal," and it reminds us of the first sin, which is the first time in the Torah where reference is made to clothing. Given this, what was Korach trying to say? He was saying that maybe the *beged* should be all *techelet*. And why? Because what if we have a world that was perfect? What if we have a world that was elevated and exalted? A world with no mistakes and no problems? A world which was full of *kedushah*?

If we think about it, the *techelet* reminds us of the sky which connects us to Hashem, and this is what Korach was saying to us: A world full of *techelet* could help us go above the nitty gritty of this world. Let's just go up to the sky with a tallit that is completely *techelet*!

So, what was Hashem's reaction to this? He said, "Korach, you don't understand. The tzitzit are so much better than a tallit full of *techelet*. A tallit full of *techelet* is something that belongs to the sky. You're searching for the stars, but you forgot the white strings."

What this means is that the beauty of the world is to be aware of the fact that the world that Hashem has given us is not something that we have to run away from. Instead, it is something we can embrace. It is something we can love. And it is something that we can be a part of. Yes, there needs to be *techelet*. Yes, there needs to be an identity. Yes, there needs to be an idea of perfection. But they need to tie together the elevated and the mundane. They need to relate to each other, and they need to speak to each other.

When Korach is swallowed up by the ground, Hashem was saying to him that you forgot the beauty which is down here. You're speaking about *techelet*; you're speaking about a world where everyone is *kadosh*, and that is all true, but it is only beautiful if it is associated with the ground and if it's linked with life.

I heard a great question from a friend of mine who said, "I can't be with my roommate anymore." I then asked him why not, and he replied, "He doesn't learn enough. It is not a great atmosphere." I was taken aback, because I was trying to understand, since when do we define a person based on the amount of time that they learn? How could it be that only the *kedushah* is what defines us?

Instead, what defines us is the idea of what the *kedushah* is doing in this world. When the ground swallowed up Korach, it was saying to stop only asking how high can you go, but start asking how relevant you are. Don't ask how much you can be a part of the sky like the *batei midrash* of the *Chachmei Atuna* from *Masechta Bava Batra* where it was flying in the air. Our *batei midrash* are grounded, and they understand that the greatest ladder of Yaakov Avinu can only go up if it remembers that it's starting from the bottom.

This is something that Korach forgot, and it is something that we need to remember; in order to have the berachah of loving life and loving the world; of recognizing that sitting with people, talking with people, having coffee with people, is not something random, but the highest level of what we are supposed to do. Like the tzitzit of *techelet* which is tied together with the world, we should be *zocheh* to believe in that, to love that, and to connect to that.

Parashat Chukat

CHOOSE AND FEEL

PARASHAT CHUKAT INTRODUCES us to many transitions: The transition from the first years of the *midbar* to the last years, the transitions between different leaderships, and the transition of Moshe Rabbeinu thinking he is going to enter Eretz Yisrael to losing Eretz Yisrael. Given all this, I would like to explore an idea from a Chassidic master of our generation named Aharon Ross. He asks a very deep question about our parashah regarding the famous story of Moshe Rabbeinu hitting the rock. The question is: Why didn't Hashem just tell Moshe to speak to the rock instead of holding the staff? If He told him to hold the staff, then it most probably would give Moshe the opportunity to fail! So why didn't Hashem tell Moshe to go without his staff and just speak to it?

In fact, this is a similar question to the one we find relating to Gan Eden. Why did Hashem give both the *Eitz HaDaat* and the *Eitz HaChaim*? Why couldn't Hashem just have given us the *Eitz HaChaim*? Why did we need to struggle with *Eitz HaDaat*? Ultimately, why did Hashem have to give us that option for failure?

I think that, although it's very challenging to fail, and it's obviously not anything that we're looking for, the idea of failure, more than the actual failure itself, is what gives us the option for choice. It gives us the opportunity to choose. Ultimately, Hashem is teaching us something very significant with the story of Moshe Rabbeinu.

Of course, we can be given everything to succeed, and we can run away from every problem. We could resolve every single struggle. We could remove every single problem in the world, and by doing so we would succeed. However, we wouldn't feel success. We might be able to avoid failure, and we might be in a place where we were transformed.

But with all of that transformation, it would not be something that would be internal or something that we would really feel.

A common question that I and my friends dealt with when going into the army was if we should go into the units that are without the secular circles of Am Yisrael, or whether we should go into the army together with the secular circle? My *imma* always taught a very deep idea that if you can't deal with the challenge, then you don't love what you're doing. In fact, my *imma* told me that you could be with the secular, you could meet the world, and you could see things that you don't usually see, but when you love something, it's not going to cause you to let go of what you love; you're only going to be able to become deeper, wider, and greater. Yes, when Moshe Rabbeinu was holding the staff there was an option for failure. But then, the speaking was so much deeper and real because he was holding the staff. Choosing words over actions is what makes the words so much deeper.

The berachah, as we go into *Parashat Chukat* as well as the week of the seventeenth of Tammuz, is that we should know that there are walls of Yerushalayim that can break. That there are many things that can go wrong. But this doesn't mean that we should limit the choices. Instead, we have to create love, and we have to infuse our relationships. And if we're really in love and connected, then obviously there is an option for failure, but we don't need to run away.

Ultimately, we learn from Moshe Rabbeinu and the journey of the people to Eretz Yisrael that when there are choices, there can be failure, but it also means that if you choose the other option you will really love the land of Eretz Yisrael.

May we be *zocheh* not to be afraid of failure, but instead, may we be aware of the fact that our failures teach us to choose to love the things that we do.

Parashat Pinchas

STRONG FOUNDATION

WHAT IS THE MOST important character trait for having a relationship with Hashem?

There are many people in the world who are searching for a relationship with Hashem, but obviously Hashem is infinite and we're finite and we don't always feel His presence. So, what is the most important character trait for someone to build a bridge between themselves and Hashem?

Answer number one could be consistency. This is because, in order for us to understand Hashem, we have to realize that Hashem is infinite, and He went against His nature by "contracting" Himself for the sake of creating humanity. What this means is that Hashem was willing to do the opposite of His essence. In contrast, our nature is to always be dynamic, and to be consistent would be to go against our nature. Therefore, if Hashem went against His nature by constricting Himself into a world that's physical—which is Hashem changing His essence in order for us to have space—then we have to go against our essence, which is always chaotic. Therefore, to build a consistent lifestyle is to really say to Hashem that we are willing to sacrifice to Hashem just like Hashem was willing to "sacrifice" for us.

Another option could be the character trait of honesty. In the Gemara, we know it says that Hashem's name is *Emet*. The word *emet*, honesty, is made up of the first, middle, and last letters of the *aleph-bet*. Being honest means that you don't only start things, you don't only end things, but you go through the whole journey from beginning to middle to end. That's what it means to be truthful. You don't just say something, but you commit to it, you act on it, you live it, and you're willing to go through that whole process. That is what Hashem's name is: *Emet*. I think that if you think about both traits, they are really saying the same thing. Truthfulness is about being consistent with your decisions, about being reliable, and not jumping all around from here to there—doing this and doing that—but not really doing anything.

A last option could be that not only do you need to know Hashem's name, which is *Emet*, and not only do you need to understand Hashem's essence, which is to go against His nature, but you also have to recognize that if it's all about you then you are trying to become a god.

When we say *Shema*, we say: "שמע ישראל ה' אלוקינו ה' אחד"—Hear, O Israel, Hashem is our God, Hashem is One." If you try and do things on your own, and you try to do things to serve yourself, then you are trying to make yourself a god and not relate to God. When you have a phone on you it's called being "self-owned" because you have become owned inside yourself.[1] As a result, whenever you are holding a phone, you can't really have a relationship with Hashem because Hashem is *echad* and not us. When we are "owned" by our phones our minds are not with Hashem. He's saying that we can't be serving other things other than Hashem.

Overall, the concept of Hashem means realizing that I'm not aware of myself, but I understand that Hashem gave me a world to be responsible for and the privilege of looking at the bigger picture.

The answer is that all three of these responses are basically all saying the same thing. Our parashah speaks about *korbanot* which are the bridge between the world and God. How do we go from an animal which is the lowest, and go all the way up to *Kodesh Hakodashim* and *Beit Hamikdash*? What is that journey like from A to B? There is one *korban* that opens up all the *korbanot* no matter what day it is, even if it's a fast day or Shabbat. Every single *chag* that we speak about in *Parashat Pinchas* ends with the same sentence: "*al olat hatamid*." If you want to bring something special such as a *korban* for Shabbat, you are only allowed to do it after the *Korban Tamid*. If you want to bring a *korban* for Yom Kippur which is very unique, you can only bring it after the

---

1   Rav Yair often mentioned this throughout yeshiva to get the guys to understand how our generation is so self-centered mainly because of our phones that "self-own" us.

Korban Tamid. The secret of the *korbanot* is that they are all founded on the *Korban Tamid.* The *Korban Tamid* represents that the greatest sacrifice we can make in building a relationship with Hashem is to be willing to commit to consistency. The *Korban Tamid* is the essence of what it means to enter into the world of Beit Hamikdash. It is a world that says that consistency is not a replacement for inspiration; it is the foundation of it. Yes, we need inspiration. Yes, we need the special. Yes, we need the different. But it needs to be founded on *Korban Tamid* which is the core, the foundation, and where it all comes from.

Parashat Ki Tetzei

OUTSIDE BUILDS INSIDE

LEARNING CONVERSATION

The parashah begins with the words *"ki tetzei"* which means "when you go out." The parashah ends with stories of *"ki tavo"* which means "when you enter." You can see that this parashah begins and ends with an issue of going in and going out. It starts off with the verb of *ki tetzei* which means to go outward, and it finishes with the verb of *ki tavo* which means coming back. The question that the *Sefat Emet* elaborates on is, Why does the parashah begin with going outward and only then ends with going inward?

To understand this question, we must first recognize that there is a big tension in the mitzvah of mezuzah. The mezuzah stands at the entrance to our homes and it's in between the outside—where we work and where we are very active in the world—and the inside—where it is quieter and it's just the family. The mezuzah, in a way, lives in between those two worlds. The interesting thing about the mezuzah is that it's placed on the outer part of the doorpost. This gives us a message which is that the greatest question for a person to ask is, what is the right way to relate outward?

We all leave our homes every day, but the question that mezuzah is asking us is a very direct question which is: How can you make sure that when you go out you are being effective, responsible, in control, and not controlled? The message of the mezuzah is the concept of realizing that the real protection that we need is going outward. Outside is something that can really pull us toward a negative space. The outside could affect us and could control us, and we put the mezuzah a little bit outward and we're saying that before you go out, you need to know why. Before

211

you go out, you need to know the purpose. Before you go to work, you need to ask yourself the question: What is the reason I am doing this? Before you learn Torah, you need to ask yourself the question: Why am I doing this? Before you walk out and you do all these different things that you do, you must be able to ask yourself the simple question of "Why?" The mezuzah teaches us that the best way to go out is to be strong and connected to oneself internally. If you first have an inside world, then when you go outside you will be affecting the world, and you will never be affected.

The parashah starts with *"ki tetzei*—when you go out" because it's saying that the first thing you need to realize about outside is that there is a *milchamah*, a war. The outside is bringing us into a mindset and a concept that is dealing with *milchamah*. The mezuzah is saying that you have to be aware of that before anything else. You have to be aware of *"ki tetzei la'milchamah*—When you take the field against your enemies."[1] This means that when you go out, there will be a war and you need to know, understand, and internalize it. You need to realize that the outside isn't what it looks like. It has struggles, and it has tensions that are all positive. *Ki tetzei* is not a problem because we want you to go out, but just know that there is a *milchamah*. The only way to go into a *milchamah* is if you start from inside. The most important moment of walking out into combat is before you go out and pass the border. My friends and I would say *Tefilat Ha'derech*. By saying this *tefillah* just before we went out, we realized why we were going out. We were going out because we had a home, and we knew where we came from. I think that this might connect to the shofar because we know that the shofar describes and explains to us how to bring Hashem into our lives. The shofar takes your inside and expands it outward. *Baruch Hashem*, I have the opportunity to blow shofar, and it makes you realize that you have to put everything that you have inside, and only then it expands. This teaches us that if there is no inside, then there is no relationship with Hashem.

---

1   *Devarim* 21:10.

My berachah for this parashah is that we start with *ki tetzei*, going out, before *ki tavo*, going in. We need to know that our homes must be aware of *ki tetzei*. The Torah we learn must be aware of *ki tetzei*. The actions we do must be aware of *ki tetzei*. There is an obligation and there is a world that needs to be affected and therefore its starts with *ki tetzei* because then your home will look different. It's not just a place that we sleep in, but it's a place that we think, dream, and visualize. *B'ezrat Hashem*, when we sit with our families this Shabbat, we should all really be able to know that our homes should change because of the outside. "*Ki tetzei la'milchamah*" is teaching us that you must first be aware of the atmosphere outside and therefore make sure that your home is strong enough and dedicated enough to enjoy the outside and to be there in the right way.

Parashat Ki Tetzei

ONE IS ALL

PARASHAT KI TETZEI opens with a famous halachah about going to war. When we think of wars, we think of countries and not people. But the parashah says, "וראית בשביה אשת יפת-תאר וחשקת בה ולקחת לך לאשה"—When you go out to war against your enemies, and you see among the captives a beautiful woman, and you desired her and took her for you as a wife."[1] The whole *pasuk* is written in the singular, and the whole parashah deals with the challenges of an individual. The parashah alerts us to the dangers of thinking only in the collective. When we over-contemplate the needs of the entire nation, we forget the needs of the individual. The parashah teaches us that although we're dealing with the big picture, our focus should be based on the needs and desires of the individual.

The Piaseczna Rebbe begins *Chovat HaTalmidim* with the *pasuk* "חנך לנער על-פי דרכו. גם כי יזקין לא יסור ממנה—Educate a child according to his ways. Even when he ages, he will not stray away from it."[2] Looking at the first two words, the Piaseczna Rebbe is hinting at a secret message. The words that Shlomo says are *"chanoch lana'ar*—educate the *child*," not *"chanoch l'na'arim*—educate the *children*." You would think the goal of education would be to teach a lot of people. However, King Shlomo and the Piaseczna Rebbe teach us that although we're dealing with the many, the orientation needs to be on the individual. If we don't realize the needs of the individual, the community becomes destructive and not productive.

---

1   *Devarim* 21:11.
2   *Mishlei* 22:6.

As we enter into *Ki Tetzei* and enter into the September 2019 Israeli elections, which is a time where we're speaking about national issues, we should realize that focusing on the needs of individuals is the best way to affect the nation.

I give a berachah to all of us that we should understand that Am Yisrael's greatest need is for us to develop ourselves so we can affect the nation as a whole.

Parashat Ki Tavo

GO DOWN THE SLIDE

ENTERING INTO KI TAVO, we struggle with *shishi*, the sixth *aliyah*. Admittedly, *shishi* is really, really long, but that's not the reason we struggle. Instead, the reason we struggle it's because what it contains is the greatest number of curses that Hashem ever gives to Am Yisrael in the Torah. Here, the curses are twice as long as those found in *Sefer Vayikra*. So, we try to say them quietly, run away from them, and in doing so, we try to skip over them.

Of course, all this is in preparation for Rosh Hashanah, and right now we are entering into Chai Elul, the eighteenth day of Elul, where we speak about the Baal Shem Tov. Given this, we will try to connect the Baal Shem Tov to this story of the curses.

Many of us look at the curses and we try to escape from them. But maybe they are written in the Torah because we have to run to them? And to address this question we must ask another: What does running to the curses mean?

The secret is that a lot of times we want to be comforted; we want to feel like everything is perfect and that everything is pink, and everything is great. (Rav Yair often refers to this as a "petting-zoo" where we like to be "pet.") This is where there's no struggle; there's no challenges; there's no darkness; there's no limits. This is our perception of what we are looking for.

Significantly, we are taught at the end of *Ki Tavo* that the greatest love that Hashem can give and show you is that you matter. And what does it mean that you matter? It means that Hashem is willing to get angry enough to show you His wrath in order to tell you that you are relevant enough for Him to pay attention to you.

In terms of human relationships, paying attention to you means that what you do matters, notwithstanding the risks involved. At the same time, when you make a mistake, others—who are paying attention to you—don't look the other way.

To use an analogy, if someone attempts to ride a bike and falls, the scab on their knee is not a sign of success or of failure. Instead, it is a sign that you tried and that you are participating. Similarly, when you're crying it means that you're feeling something, and you are involved in something, because no one cries simply from being a spectator. And similarly, when you get to a wedding and you know the reality and the struggles of life, and you know the challenges that needed to be overcome to reach that moment, then you are more likely to cry. My *imma* cried a lot at my wedding because she saw the entire journey. She was participating in all the things that took place until I reached that moment, and this is what we learn from the Baal Shem Tov.

The Baal Shem Tov was able to reach high levels of spirituality because he was able to experience pain. The Baal Shem Tov saw a generation falling apart; he saw a generation after Shabbtai Tzvi, and he saw the scholars who were teaching, and no one was listening. Yet the Baal Shem Tov said that he was not afraid of being there in the forest. He was one of the "medical people" who saw "broken legs and broken arms" and it was from there, that very place, that he created *Chassidut.* "Chai Elul," the eighteenth of Elul, is the birthday (in 1698) of the founder of Chassidism, Rabbi Yisrael Baal Shem Tov. It is also the day on which his "spiritual grandson," the founder of Chabad, Rabbi Schneur Zalman of Liadi, was born, in 1745. The idea of Chai Elul is about celebrating the path of the Baal Shem Tov and what it means for someone to not be afraid of what's real. This is what it means to be involved in life.

The berachah of *Ki Tavo*, of preparing us for Rosh Hashanah, especially following a year that has been paralyzed by the challenges of Corona, is that we need to face the fact that we have many scabs we have to deal with: Scabs of loneliness, scabs of distance, scabs of not being able to plan anything, scabs of a world that is not the way we want it to be. But we can't run away from the scabbed world.

Someone showed me an article saying that the greatest education is scabbed legs. We've been taught that everyone should be perfect, and nowadays, our playgrounds are made of plastic and their flooring is softer, so no one gets hurt. But we have also lost that experience of a scabbed leg.

As we prepare ourselves for a new year, we should prepare ourselves to take risks, to get involved, and to ride on the slide. We should remember that we grow because we try, and that our muscles are strengthened by the efforts we make. Ultimately, what we learn from this parashah is that rather than scabs just representing pain, they also represent gain as well.

MOADIM

Rosh Hashanah

CELEBRATING DOUBT

WE'RE OBVIOUSLY all feeling the intensity of Rosh Hashanah. The date of Rosh Hashanah is the first (and second) of Tishrei, and according to the Gemara it is a time where something really important happens. But what is the "important thing" that happens on the first day of the month?

There is a transition from being revealed to being covered. The moon, at least for many of us, is something that is abstract and far away from us. But really, it is at the center of the Jewish people, it resembles the Jewish people, and its journey is the journey of the Jewish people.

The moon, in the middle of the month, reveals its light and its clarity, and its radiance makes us feel that even though there is darkness, there is still something to hold onto. But then, from the middle until the beginning of a new month, the moon transitions from revealing itself to hiding itself; it goes from a state of giving hope with its light, to representing doubt with its hiddenness.

What this means is that Rosh Hashanah is a day that celebrates doubt rather than hope, and understandably, this is a difficult message with which to begin a new year.

In general, everyone loves sending messages of hope and excitement for the new year. However, I don't think anyone is saying, "I don't know if you'll have a good year." Nevertheless, the day that we celebrate is when the revelation of the moon is hidden and covered; the moon is communicating a message of doubt and challenging us to deal with doubt. The obvious question is, why is that a way to start the new year?

A possible answer to this question is that when things are clear we feel irrelevant, we don't fully engage and involve ourselves, because we already know how things are going to end up. The idea of Rosh Hashanah, however, is that we should fully engage, we should get fully involved, and we should know that our actions will make a difference.

Understood this way, the berachah that we should have when going into a new year is that we should celebrate the doubts that we've been given as a message from God that we can fully engage, we can be fully involved, we can make a difference, and even if we just see ourselves as a pawn in a larger game of chess, the steps we take can have a big impact. *Shanah tovah*!

Rosh Hashanah

LOOKING FORWARD

"The only way to lift the past is to envision the future."

LEARNING CONVERSATION

There are three big days that start off the Jewish Calendar: Two days of Rosh Hashanah, and one day of Yom Kippur. Our nature is to look at things from a plane's view and see everything as the same. But to truly love something means to become aware of the minor details that create an individual identity for each experience, person, or holiday in this case. We often don't realize that there is a huge difference between Rosh Hashanah and Yom Kippur. As an example, I remember Rosh Hashanah when I was studying at Yeshivat Otniel. We would start davening at 5:00 a.m. and finish at around 3:00 p.m. We would eat for an hour and sleep a little bit and then the next day again, we would daven from 5:00 a.m. until 3:00 p.m. Yom Kippur was basically the same. They felt like three full days of davening—the mindsets were similar—they were three days of awe, so much so that one time, my friend said to me, "Yair, davening on Rosh Hashanah and Yom Kippur is the same thing—just one has a snack in the middle."

If you really think about it, however, they are very different, and only by learning the difference can we really have a deep relationship with each one.[1]

---

1   There is also a big difference between the first and second day of Rosh Hashanah, but we won't speak about that in this *shiur*.

I want to try to understand the difference in the context by asking one big question: How is it possible for change to last? These days we all think and hope for change—not only to change what has been done wrong, but to also elevate what has been done well. But what makes an experience of change become everlasting?

To try to understand the core of long-term change, I want to share a story that happened this week. Tuesday night, I heard about the tragedy of Jonny Lax passing away. On Motzaei Shabbat, I got onto a flight to his sister's wedding with Becky that was being held during the *shivah*. There were so many thoughts in my mind going to the wedding. I was able to speak to Rebbi Michael, Jonny's *abba*, just before the wedding, while he was sitting *shivah*. Rebbi Michael said, "Yair, it's really important to change the mindset and just focus on the wedding."

So, this concept of Rebbi Michael got me thinking. How can someone really change his mindset? How can someone change on Rosh Hashanah?

This sentence of Rebbi Michael can bring us back to the difference between Rosh Hashanah and Yom Kippur. One of the main differences between the davening on Rosh Hashanah and Yom Kippur is that on Rosh Hashanah we don't speak about sins. We don't say, "*Ashamnu, bagadnu, gazalnu*," nor "*al chet she'chatanu*." Essentially, there is no mention of sin at all. On Yom Kippur, however, the focus of the davening is very much on the concept of what we did wrong. So, although both Rosh Hashanah and Yom Kippur embody a strong element of *tefillah*, on Rosh Hashanah, the prayers are not about remembering the sins that we did during the past year and not about *teshuvah*. Rosh Hashanah is about creating an understanding of Hashem being our King and deciding that during the next year that we want to believe in Hashem and his endless light.

On a simple level, the message of Rosh Hashanah is that before you look backward, you have to look forward. But, Rosh Hashanah is the first day of the year, and it seems like maybe we should be looking back on all the mistakes we made. But instead of asking, "What did I do right and what did I do wrong?" we look forward and ask, "Where do I want to go?"

The focus of Rosh Hashanah is on what it means to have a relationship with Hashem and what it really means for Hashem to be part of our lives and part of our world. Only after we look forward can we think about all the mistakes we made during the past year. The deep message of Rosh Hashanah is to look forward, and the deep message of Yom Kippur is to look backward. The strength of the connection of the future vision that gives us the inspiration to confront our wrongdoings. Interestingly, first we look forward. Before we focus on what we did wrong, we need to be aware of where we are headed. Rosh Hashanah teaches us: Yes, you made mistakes, but what is your destination? Only afterward should you think about your mistakes and the things you want to fix.

When Michael told me about changing one's mindset, when I got the berachah and the privilege to be at the wedding, the biggest berachah Michael gave me was the idea of looking at Rami, looking at Rebecca, and looking at the family, and asking, "What does the future hold?" As I danced with the *chatan*, I tried to think about the future, although after the wedding, I was aware of all the pain of the past.

Sometimes, the only way to enable change is to remember that Rosh Hashanah comes before Yom Kippur.

As we sit with our families on the last Shabbat of the year, twenty-four hours before Rosh Hashanah, we should try to really focus on that one question: "Where do we want to go?" We should try not to look at our mistakes and what we did wrong, but rather, contemplate where we want to go. In that way, when we do confront our mistakes, it will be from a much more positive and productive place.

Rosh Hashanah

WHAT DO YOU WANT?

WE ARE ENTERING the week before Rosh Hashanah, and I want to share some Torah from *mori v'rabi*, my Rabbi and teacher, Rav Re'em, which was taught to me by Rav Ari Baruch. We all know, and we grew up being taught, that Rosh Hashanah is the day when we crown Hashem as our King. However, what is interesting is the way we do it—by blowing the shofar. But what is so significant, so unique, and so powerful about this blasting of sound, that it suddenly makes Hashem our King?

It simply comes down to a very basic concept that everything that happens in this world starts with desire. An action does not begin with the action; it starts with a desire. This desire is always from Hashem. Yet, anything that is willed by Hashem does not change. For example, Shabbat was created by Hashem, separate from our existence, and it therefore never changes. Shabbat is always on the seventh day; we cannot cook, change, or affect the world. Instead, we only are there to receive, which is why Shabbat starts with *Kabbalat Shabbat*, because it is not based on us, it is based on Hashem. Another example is *Torah She'bichtav*, the Written Torah. This Torah was written by Hashem, and it cannot be changed or affected; it is the desire of Hashem, and therefore it never changes.

When we look at the other aspect, at things whose desires come from man, we can see that they always change. For example, Yom Tov was established by man, and as a result, it is something that will always be on a different day of the week. On one occasion Yom Tov might be on Shabbat, another time Monday, another Tuesday, etc. This is because things that stem from us need to change consistently. Another example is *Torah She'baal Peh*, the Oral Torah. According to *Masechta Chagigah*,

226

divrei Torah, words of Torah, are being renewed on a daily basis because they stem from us.[1]

What is so unique about the shofar is that it sets the entire mindset of Rosh Hashanah. There are many days of the year that are dependent on Hashem, and many experiences where we wait for Hashem. Many things are entirely out of our hands. Rosh Hashanah is different. The shofar has fifteen different sounds; it is always changing, and the sounds of the shofar are blown in different orders. This too connects to the idea that the shofar is dependent on us. The idea of Rosh Hashanah is not just that Hashem is King. Instead, there are elements that stem from us because they are based on our desires.

On the first day of the year, we must ask ourselves a simple question: Are we really expressing our desires and asking for it? My children are truly amazing, and Adiel is here taking the video. But if Adiel wants chocolate and candy, but does not ask me for it, I will not know that is what he wants and so I will not give it to him. Rosh Hashanah is not about seeing that Hashem as scary or merely recognizing that He is the Master of the Universe. Instead, it is also about realizing that our relationship with Hashem is dependent on what we are asking, looking for, and what we are envisioning.

---

1   3a.

Sukkot

FROM THIRTEEN TO SEVEN

SUKKOT IS A CHAG that contains so many transformative ideas, but one of the ideas we want to focus on is the *korbanot*. We know that the *korbanot* of all the holidays are consistent. For example, if we look at Pesach specifically, we bring the same *korban* every single day. However, when we look at Sukkot this consistency changes. First, we bring thirteen, then the next day twelve, and the day after that eleven, and we end up finishing with a total of seven *korbanot* on the last day of Sukkot. Here we can see that Sukkot is about being dynamic, transformative, and being a part of nature. The question that I had is why do we start the *chag* with specifically thirteen and finish with seven? If the idea behind it is about transformation, we could have started from seven and went to one, or maybe we could have started with one hundred and gone to ninety-three. Why is it *davka* thirteen to seven? There is an idea that if you add all the numbers up it comes out to a total of seventy, which is connected to the seventy nations of the world, but I think that there might be a secret within the numbers thirteen and seven.

If we remember how it is during the last moments of Yom Kippur, during *Neilah*, it is very repetitive. It is just focused on one thing and that is the Thirteen Attributes of Mercy, the *Yud-Gimmel Middos*. As a result, we ended off Yom Kippur with the number thirteen. But still, what is the message of the *korbanot* where we begin with thirteen—where we ended off on Yom Kippur—and go from there until seven? What Sukkot is saying to Yom Kippur is that thirteen is a means, but it's not the goal. The idea is that Sukkot has a "conversation" with Yom Kippur saying that thirteen might be where you ended off, but we need something greater. We need to go from thirteen back to seven.

Obviously, there are seven days of the week which resemble reality. Seven is the world of the week where things operate according to nature. The journey of Sukkot from the number thirteen is that we were so exalted, we were so above, but we come to recognize all of this as just a means. We received the opportunity and the privilege of moving from our angel selves (Yom Kippur) back to the reality of our regular selves (Sukkot). So many people love talking about dreams, but the real question to ask is: Do you realize that the goal of a dream is to infuse reality? We dream at night only so that we have a new energy during the day.

My berachah as we enter into Sukkot is that we should realize that right now we are living in the world of thirteen. We are living in the world of seclusion and separation, and we are removed from reality. We have nothing to do with each other and we can't do *chessed*. At least in the Land of Israel, we can't have a regular Sukkot because we are in isolation, we are stuck in lockdown, and things are not involved in reality. Our *tefillah* this Sukkot, as we descend from thirteen all the way back to seven is to look at ourselves and say, "Yes, we have received Yom Kippur. We have received the opportunity to live with our families in isolation. We have received this idea of demanding of ourselves." But this Sukkot our berachah, our plea, and our demand of ourselves is to go from the exalted and separated thirteen—which in the pandemic there is obviously a negative separation, but there also exists a positive separation. This separation of living in the world of thirteen and Yom Kippur is only a means. It enables us to infuse the real world that we are yearning for and searching for with what's being presented in Sukkot.

Simchat Torah

LIFTING

WHEN WE GO into Simchat Torah there's obviously a big question. The big question that we have is, what is so unique about dancing around the Torah? We could understand that if you're reading it, you get excited. We could understand that if you are learning it, you get excited. It also makes sense that if you're having a *shiur*, you may feel inspired. But to go around in circles with a closed *Sefer Torah*, how is that so significant? How is that so essential? And we can even see this question even deeper when we compare it to Shavuot. On Shavuot we celebrate the learning of the Torah. We learn all night and we understand the depth of what it means to learn Torah. But what does it mean to dance around the Torah? I think we can understand it if we connect it to the sukkah.

The sukkah starts with the letter *samech*, which looks like a circle. The whole idea of the sukkah is that we are surrounded. We are surrounded by Hashem's reality. We look up at the *s'chach*, the branches placed on the roof of the sukkah, and we see a bit of the sky. We look down, and we see we're outside, so we see the ground. So, we are surrounded by the light of the reality that Hashem gave us. The idea of a sukkah is that it is something like a *samech*—it's an experience that surrounds you. It is that you are surrounded and that you feel you are in the womb and that you feel Hashem's embrace. But the real question of Sukkot is what do you do with that? What do you do with that love? What do you do with that surrounding? Do you surround Hashem? Or do you stop there? And the idea of Simchat Torah is that we have to realize that Hashem has surrounded us. He has given us Rosh Hashanah. He has given us Yom Kippur. And He has given us Sukkot. We have been surrounded by so much depth and so much opportunity. But the big question of Simchat Torah relates to the fact that this is the final day of this series of *Yamim Tovim*. Just before we head into the winter you've been surrounded, but are you willing to surround others? You've been given, but are you willing to give to others? Hashem has given you the sukkah, but are you willing to be *His* sukkah and surround *His* Torah?

My berachah as we go into Simchat Torah is that we should understand the beauty of not only what it means to learn, but also what it means to live a lifestyle wherein we recognize that not only do we need the Torah, but that the Torah needs us. This is why we surround the Torah in order to make a statement to ourselves that it's not only that we were uplifted by the Torah, but that we need to lift *it* up. That we need to take the Torah and take it to a new level and to a new creation. *B'ezrat Hashem* we should all be *zocheh* this Simchat Torah to not only realize what people do for us, and what the Torah does for us, but that we get the strength, the energy, and the excitement to give, create, build, and to surround not only others, but also Hashem.

Purim

NOT YOUR STORY

LEARNING CONVERSATION

I wanted to learn together two words from *Megillat Esther*. Esther came up to Mordechai, and after hearing about the fact that every single Jew was slated to be murdered, she said to him, "*V'tzumu alai*—Fast for me."[1] I want to try and understand what Esther was really saying when she said this.

I had the greatest privilege to fly with the Ohr Chaim basketball team to a tournament in Florida, and on Sunday we were in the finals playing against Katz Yeshiva High School. If I would have said to my players just before the game that I brought in a few new players to play instead of them, they would all said to me, "Rav Yair, you are crazy!"

Esther stood at a momentous time in her life and in the history of Jewish people. I would have said to Esther that if you want to fast, then fast, but don't tell other people to fast for you. Clearly, Esther was planning to fast with everyone else, but what did it mean that she was asking the Jewish people to fast for her? It was her game, and her responsibility, so what does that mean, "Fast for me"?

Even more than this, even if Esther really believed that they needed to fast, why didn't she tell them to "fast for Hashem"? Repent, change, and do it for Hashem. But to say they should do it for her? On another level, if you want to say it's important from them to fast, maybe tell them to "fast for yourselves"? Fast for the fact that all of you are about to be murdered. What made Esther specifically say these words of

---

1   *Esther* 4:16.

"*V'tzumu alai*—Fast for me"? It's like almost letting go of the game and letting someone else play the game for her.

I think the answer is that Esther understood that in life there are problems, but there are also things that cause problems. We live in a world of results. I was giving out report cards, and I was giving people results. My kids come home with results—just before the end of registration for yeshiva next year—and you know that everyone is only thinking about results. Esther was saying to the Jewish people: Your orientation of results is the problem. You need to understand what the cause is. What caused Am Yisrael to reach a level where they could all be dancing at a party while the *Menorah* was being presented in front of people who were desecrating and disrespecting it? How could that have happened? Esther's answer to this is very simple: It is essentially that when your whole mindset is about you, then you are able to let go of everything that is truly meaningful in life. Esther said to the Jewish people: Don't fast for the murder, but fast for the cause. All of you were all focused on your personal development but no other people's development. This is why she says, "*V'tzumu alai*—Fast for me." For the first time, live in a context and in a mindset that someone else comes before you.

I am boarding a plane in twenty-four hours with my two sons, Ohr Eytan, who is nine, and Adiel, who is six. We are flying to Israel and making a project for Shalva. The project that they are making involves asking themselves: Am I willing to think about someone else before I think about myself? It is important to think about yourself, but it can't be first. You need to see yourself first as someone who is aware of others. This is why Esther said, "*V'tzumu alai*—Fast for me." She wanted them to stop being so egocentric and selfish, and to start living with an awareness of someone other than themselves.

I want to connect this to one more thing to Purim. The two mitzvot that I want to focus on are *mishloach manot* and *matanot l'evyonim*. They both have seemingly nothing to do with the holiday of Purim. Imagine someone walking through the desert and suddenly, he remembers that it's Pesach. If he has matzah in his bag, he can keep the mitzvah of Pesach. If it is Chanukah and he has a small tent, he could light the candles. But if you are in the desert all alone, you can't do the mitzvah of *mishloach manot*. If you are in the desert all alone, you can't do *matanot l'evyonim*. So maybe, when Esther says "*V'tzumu alai,*" we become aware of something bigger than just ourselves. It is the same reason that we do the mitzvah of *mishloach manot* and *matanot l'evyonim*, because you can't do them by yourself, and this is the definition of Purim.

I give us all a berachah that as we enter into this *yom* of *Kodesh Hakodashim*—the day which is the aspect of the Holy of Holies—that we start realizing that our best story is when we are aware of another story. We must realize that our lives cannot be just our jobs, our salaries, and our grades. If they are, then there is no reason for Amalek not to come back. That is why when we enter into this Purim, we should give *mishloach manot* with tears and with a dance, knowing that another person is letting me fulfill the mitzvot of Purim. When we give the *matanot l'evyonim* twice, we should look at that person and say to them: It is *you* that has built Purim *for me*, and without you I cannot fulfill the mitzvot of this day. I know that I can't keep Purim without my family, and I want to *mamash* thank my wife and children for making me know that the greatest story, is when it's not just your story.

Pesach

WE DIDN'T EARN REDEMPTION

ONE OF THE fundamental themes of the Seder is והגדת לבנך, telling the story of the Exodus to our children. So, my son, Ohr Eytan, will ask a few questions and we'll try to answer them.

1. Why are there specifically four cups of wine at the Seder?
2. Why are there specifically ten plagues?
3. The Haggadah says, "והיו מספרים ביציאת מצרים כל אותו הלילה עד שבאו תלמידיהם ואמרו להם רבותינו הגיע זמן קריאת שמע של שחרית—They were telling the story of the Exodus from Egypt that whole night, until their students came and said to them, 'The time of [reciting] the morning *Shema* has arrived.'" So, why do we have to stop telling the story at the beginning of *z'man k'riat Shema*?

The Piaseczna Rebbe answers the third question. If they had to stop because of *k'riat Shema*, they could have waited another three hours. So, the reason they stopped was because the students came in. The rabbis were telling the story all night to themselves, without students. There was no continuation of the story, no younger generation to hear what happened. When the students came in, the rabbis realized that all the bad things that we went through in Egypt would end—because the students came in. They had someone to tell the story of our redemption to. Once the students arrived, they knew the story of Am Yisrael would continue, so they didn't need to mourn anymore.

Now, back to the first two questions. The four cups teach us that things that are important take time. Sometimes, Ohr Eytan and I make dinner together. But dinner tastes better if we took more time to make it. What Hashem is teaching is that things that are special take time.

235

It's the same idea with the Ten Plagues. Hashem could have taken us out after one plague. But once we had more than one plague, it became clear that Hashem was taking us out to teach us a lesson. We have more cups and more plagues to teach us that just one wasn't enough. The Exodus was a process, and we need to be aware of that on Seder night.

We all clean our homes before Pesach, something that takes a lot of time. So, the idea of cleaning is that the most important thing in life is the home. That's why we spend a lot of time cleaning it.

My berachah as we enter into the Seder is that through any of these lessons, we can learn that the more important something is, the more time it takes. We should focus the majority of our time on things that matter. We can all do things that are fun, but we need to make sure that we spend the majority of our time on the priorities of life.

Pesach

LOOK IN, NOT AT

WHEN WE ENTER into *shevi'i shel Pesach*, the seventh day of Pesach, it is very obvious that we need to enter into the world of water. The experience of *Yam Suf* was the world of water. The message we should have when we enter into the last day of Pesach is one of trying to realize that the first experience of the Jewish people, the first action we experienced as a nation—before *maamad Har Sinai* and even before *Marah* when we received the mitzvah of Shabbat—was seeing the sea split and realizing that this was how Hashem wanted to save us.

Before we try to understand exactly what happened at *Yam Suf* and why it was so significant, it is important to realize how essential water was in *yetziat Mitzrayim*.

If we go back to the beginning of the exile, it started with throwing the Jews into the Nile river. Then the redeemer of the Jewish people, Moshe Rabbeinu, was redeemed from the water. When Moshe Rabbeinu found his wife, it was at a well. If we look at the *makkot*, they begin with water being made into blood. We end off this journey at *k'riat Yam Suf*, and this experience, too, is connected with water. There is something essential in this message of water that Hashem was trying to reveal to the Jewish people.

What might this message be? One of the messages could be that if we look at the letters of *mayim*, (מים), water, it begins and ends the same letter. It starts with a *mem* and ends with a *mem sofit*, but in the middle there is a letter *yud*. What is interesting is that this is exactly what water does; it reveals the inner potential. For example, if water is poured onto a computer, it will not survive, because it does not have an inner soul, an inner potential. But if one pours water onto a seed, it will thrive, as the message of a seed is that it is trying to analyze what is going on inside. That is the biology of what the water is about.

If we look at what happened at *Yam Suf*, the water suddenly split into two. We have the letter *mem* on each side. Then in the middle, where Hashem is, we walk through. I think that we need to look at water as something that has an inner potential and that it is necessary for things to be revealed. This is like asking, "Where is Hashem?" When we consider how Am Yisrael left Egypt and how they needed to suddenly live in a world of Godliness, it begs the question as to how they would connect to Him. God will not be performing ten *makkot* a day, so how will they find him? Suddenly then, the water split open, and whatever one thought was once on the surface is ripped open. They soon realize that there is a *yud* inside; Hashem is inside. When they were busy looking on the surface, they did not see Hashem there. Yet, when they were faced with the sea they yelled to Moshe, not to Hashem.

We learn from this that when one sees the world on a superficial level, he will not find Hashem, relationships, and connections. Hashem's first message to the Jewish people at *Yam Suf* was not just to look at the water, but to understand it, to realize that His first message to us was that we can only build a relationship with Him by recognizing the external and the internal. The concept of Godliness is about being willing to look inside. Are we willing to look not just at something, but into something? This is what makes relationships.

We know that at the chuppah the *chatan* and *kallah* stand looking at each other. They obviously know what the other person looks like already, yet, what is really going on is that they so badly want to find a *yud*. They know how they look, they know what the *mem* is, and what the outside is, but the message of the chuppah is that they're looking at each other to be able to find what is going on beneath the surface. I know that all of us have been inside for so long.

I was *zocheh* to be in quarantine in the Old City for thirty-four days. A lot of us have big questions. But my berachah to all of us as we enter into *shevi'i shel Pesach*, into *k'riat Yam Suf*, is that we realize that Hashem's first message to Am Yisrael is that if you want to make a relationship last, you need to have patience, the stamina, and the excitement. You need to realize that the externality is teaching us that there is always something beneath it, and that you have to choose to look for it. This might be the secret of water in *yetziat Mitzrayim*, and in its climax in *k'riat Yam Suf*. *Shevi'i shel Pesach sameach*, and *b'ezrat Hashem* we should soon merit to the *geulah sh'leimah*, the complete redemption.

Shavuot

THE JOURNEY TO TORAH

THERE IS AN IDEA that "time is of the essence." This really means that timing defines experiences. We can see in Am Yisrael's holidays that the timing is not secondary; rather, it is actually the definition of the holiday. One example is Pesach. The Torah says "שמור את חדש האביב—Observe the month of *aviv*," which means that Pesach always has to come in the springtime.[1] By Pesach being in the spring, it shows us that the idea of the holiday is defined by its timing. This connects to the notion that just as the Jewish people left from slavery in the springtime, so too the world, which has just experienced winter, needs to leap out and experience redemption. Therefore, the timing really defines the essence of Pesach, and it is not only the people of Am Yisrael who need redemption, but the entire world as well.

This also connects to the *Chag HaShavuot*. It is very important to realize that the opening two words of *maamad Har Sinai* related to the timing of the experience. It starts with *"ba'chodesh hashlishi*, in the third month."[2] We don't see the mentioning of the third month anywhere else in the Torah; it does not seem significant. So, what would be the reason for the emphasis that the experience of *maamad Har Sinai* occurred in the third month? Moreover, in *Masechta Shabbat* it says that the idea of *maamad Har Sinai* is that it was given in the third month, to the nation of three books, and the children of three fathers.[3] It focuses

---

1   *Devarim* 16:1.
2   *Shemot* 19:1.
3   88a.

on the concept that it was specifically in the third month. What is the significance?

The *Sefat Emet* teaches that the word "*chodesh,*" month, is also similar to the word *chadash*, new; this signifies that the month is the idea of renewal. The renewal of the moon is called Rosh Chodesh because there is a "new moon." This is the idea of what *chodesh shlishi*, the third month, means; it is also *chiddush shlishi*, a new third, that *maamad Har Sinai* is the third renewal.

Practically speaking, there are three new things that Hashem gives to the world. The first new thing is the universe, and it was created with Ten Utterances. Next is *yetziat Mitzrayim*, where Hashem created the nation. Here too, we find the idea of ten, with the ten *makkot*. The third *chiddush* is the giving of the Torah. The idea of *chodesh shlishi* is not only that it is in the third month, but this concept of the third new idea that the world needs. Why is this so significant? It is so significant because it changes the entire idea of Torah learning.

Many people think that the Torah stands alone, and that this might even be the goal. However, we learn that the Torah waited for twenty-six generations before it was given to the world. Why? The reason is that the idea of the Torah is a build-off. It is something that needs two things in order for it to be healthy and positive. The first *chiddush* is the world. If a person is not aware, involved, caring about, effecting, and learning from the world, the Torah is not what it is supposed to be. The second *chiddush*, *yetziat Mitzrayim*, is that you are part of a nation. Therefore, if you do not know the story of the nation and are not learning the history of the Jewish people, then the giving of the Torah is insignificant. It is based on the story of a nation; it is not a textbook. Only then can you receive the Torah.

For so many of us, the Torah is something that we randomly learn. The first two words of *maamad Har Sinai* are *ba'chodesh hashlishi*. The Torah needs preparation. It needs something called *sheloshet yemei hagbalah*—three days of preparation, *d'Orayta*. There is no other holiday that one is required to prepare in advance for. It might be nice, but it is not required. On Shavuot, it is needed, because it is the definition of Torah. That the Torah is something that is a continuation of other things. So too with the name of the holiday. The name of the holiday is Shavuot, which means "weeks." It is a build off of something else. Our Torah learning needs to be an extension, and not in exchange.

My berachah as we go into Shavuot is that we should merit to be able to learn from the world, to be aware of the world, to look out our windows, as we all are forced to sit inside this Shavuot. We should be able to understand the story, to sit down for an hour and learn a piece of the history of the Jewish people. Then, we can truly merit the Torah. We should all be *zocheh* not to use the Torah as an exchange, but to use it as an extension from the things that are needed in order for the Torah to be healthy. This Shavuot should be deep, real and significant for all of Am Yisrael, and the world.

ABOUT THE AUTHOR

RAV YAIR HALEVI EISENSTOCK is the Rosh Yeshiva of Yeshivat Torah V'Avodah–Chovat HaTalmidim in Jerusalem. Since assuming the role in 2018, he has inspired hundreds of young adults to look at Torah as a means to engage and have a relationship with the world around them.

Rav Yair previously worked with Kol HaNearim, which brings American high schoolers to Israel for the summer to work with at-risk children in different homes across the country. He also taught at Yeshivat Or Chaim in Toronto and Yeshivat Orayta in the Old City. He attended Yeshivat Otniel and learned under Rav Re'em HaCohen and Rav Menachem Froman.

He currently lives with his wife, Tanya, and children, Ohr Eytan, Adiel, and Roni, in Efrat.